The Gift of European Thought and the Cost of Living

THE GIFT OF EUROPEAN THOUGHT AND THE COST OF LIVING

Vassos Argyrou

berghahn
NEW YORK · OXFORD
www.berghahnbooks.com

First edition published in 2013 by

Berghahn Books

www.berghahnbooks.com

© 2013, 2017 Vassos Argyrou
First paperback edition published in 2017

All rights reserved. Except for the quotation of short passages
for the purposes of criticism and review, no part of this book
may be reproduced in any form or by any means, electronic or
mechanical, including photocopying, recording, or any information
storage and retrieval system now known or to be invented,
without written permission of the publisher.

Library of Congress Cataloging-in-Publication Data

Argyrou, Vassos.
  The gift of European thought and the cost of living / Vassos Argyrou.
    pages cm
  Includes bibliographical references and index.
  ISBN 978-1-78238-017-7 (hardback : alk. paper) — ISBN 978-1-78533-525-9 (paperback) — ISBN 978-1-78238-018-4 (ebook)
  1. Thought and thinking. 2. Enlightenment. 3. Cost and standard of living—Europe. I. Title.
  BF441.A644 2013
  153.4'2094—dc23

2013004629

British Library Cataloguing in Publication Data

A catalogue record for this book is available from the British Library

ISBN: 978-1-78238-017-7 hardback
ISBN: 978-1-78533-525-9 paperback
ISBN: 978-1-78238-018-4 ebook

For
Lisa and Nefeli
and in memory of
Christodoulos Argyrou

Contents

Chapter 1. The Circle ... 1

Chapter 2. The Gift of European Thought ... 10
The Postcolonial   10
The Take on/of the Gift   25
The Power of Giving   32

Chapter 3. The Economy of Thought ... 41
The Phenomenon and the Phantom   41
'Think for Yourself'   54
The Socialisation of Thought   62

Chapter 4. Political Economy ... 79
Re-volution   79
The Hegemonic   91
Identity Politics   99

Chapter 5. The Cost of Living ... 111
Thinking and Not Thinking   111
The Modern and the Traditional   117
The Cost of Living   125

References ... 131

Index ... 134

CHAPTER I

THE CIRCLE

The Kula is probably the best known and most celebrated anthropological example of the gift. It is also a graphic (in the double sense of the term) example of a certain circle in which the gift is implicated – a 'ring', says Malinowski, that forms a 'closed circuit'. Yet this is not the only circle here. There is another that is prior to and much more fundamental than any ring of the kind that Malinowski describes. It is the circle of the gift itself – the gift's own circularity.

The Kula is a form of exchange carried out by 'communities inhabiting a wide *ring* of islands, which form a *closed circuit*' (Malinowski 1922: 81; my emphases). It involves the circulation of necklaces of red shell – *souvala* – with bracelets of white shell – *mwali* – which as they are exchanged move around this ring in opposite directions, clockwise and anti-clockwise, respectively. And they move around it constantly, says Malinowski, on account of a certain rule. 'One transaction does not finish the Kula relationship, the rule being "once in the Kula, always in the Kula" and a partnership between two men is a permanent and *lifelong* affair' (my emphasis). Likewise the necklaces and bracelets exchanged 'may always be found travelling and changing hands, and there is no question of [their] ever settling down, so that the principle "once in the Kula, always in the Kula" applies also to the valuables themselves' (Malinowski 1922: 81–83). It is as if both the partners engaged in this exchange and the objects with which they engage one another are caught up in the circle, are surrounded by it, and cannot escape. It is as if they are destined to go round and round in circles until the end – the death of one of the partners in these lifelong relationships or the end as social death – the 'loss of face', becoming nobody (an oxymoron, no doubt), which, as Mauss says in his own discussion of the gift, is the fate of all those who fail to reciprocate.

Such is the rule of the Kula, but for all we know it may be the rule of much more than this native institution. It may even be the rule of life itself. We will therefore take the risk of paraphrasing this rule and suggesting what may sound trivial or unintelligible because much needs to be demonstrated for its import to become apparent: Once in time, always in time – always, that is, until the end of one's time – all claims to the contrary, whether implicit or explicit, notwithstanding. We will take the risk also of pointing out that if such is the case, and on account of this rule, there is no question of anyone or anything ever settling down, that whatever is caught up in time is destined to travel around the circle constantly – until the end of its time, as we have just said. We are already suggesting that time, the circle of the gift and a range of other circular phenomena – the life cycle, for example, but also, as we shall see, other circles within this circle – are inextricably intertwined. It is one of the tasks of this book to trace and highlight the connections.

It may take up to ten years for a bracelet or necklace to make the round, says Malinowski, but it always does come back to the point of departure. It stands to reason, of course. As the saying has it, what goes round, comes round. Yet Malinowski's point is not one of rationality and common sense. He has a different agenda. Being an anthropologist, he wishes to do what all anthropologists strive to do, namely, to save the 'savage'[1] – in this particular case, save it from the calumny of pure economic nature. What Malinowski wishes to do in making an issue of the Kula is to undermine the claims of those who 'reason incorrectly thus':

> The passion of acquiring, the loathing to lose or give away, is the most fundamental and most primitive element in man's attitude to wealth. In primitive man, this primitive characteristic will appear in its simplest and purer form. *Grab and never let go* will be the guiding principle of his life (Malinowski 1922: 96).

For Malinowski 'grab and never let go' is hardly what happens with this particular primitive man. He emphasises the circle of these gift exchanges precisely because he wishes to demonstrate that the Trobrianders are people like us, that they have social codes and rules which they diligently observe, that they, too, have managed to master the most primitive elements of human nature by means of culture. In fact, he will go on to argue – and this is his main point – that when it comes to attitudes to wealth, they have mastered nature to a far greater extent than we have. The gift goes round and round precisely because they always let go of what they grab. The Trobrianders may wish to possess things, but with them, says Malinowski, this desire to possess is not at all a desire to possess. Paradoxically, they wish to possess only to dispossess themselves. They take what is given to them, not to keep and appropriate but to give to someone else. Such is the ethos of this society. 'The *important point* is that with them to *possess is to give* – and here the natives differ from us notably' (Malinowski 1922: 97; my emphases).

I have highlighted the equalisation of *taking* (possession) with *giving* because it is, indeed, an important point, perhaps one of the most important points that one can make. It is important not for the reasons that Malinowski had in mind – to demonstrate the generosity of the Trobrianders – for as we shall see there is no generosity involved here (cf. Weiner 1992) or anywhere else for that matter. It is important rather because it opens up a new domain of inquiry that, although it may not necessarily lead anywhere, could perhaps shed different light on these issues. We may note two interrelated themes in this respect. The first is the implication that to give any of these ceremonial objects, the Trobriaders must first take. If 'with them to possess is to give', it stands to reason that they are always dispossessed, that they have nothing to give except what they take. Looking at it from another perspective, they must take to give because they are not themselves the creators of these objects. As Malinowski makes clear in his comparison with the British Crown jewels, the bracelets and necklaces have value because of their history, their association with mythical ancestors, heroes, or gods. They have been passed down to them through the generations and they in turn will pass them on to the next. To generalise even more, at the limit they – the Trobrianders – as much as anyone else, must take to give because no one ever makes anything (a) present from nothing. It is impossible. Any way one looks at it then, giving presupposes taking, and this is an irreducible condition. If that is the case, however, the Trobrianders, as much as anyone else, give what they do not have (for it does not belong to them) hence give nothing or, what is yet another way of saying the same thing, they give what is not and cannot be a gift.

The second and related theme has to do with the equalisation of the two notions we have highlighted – taking and giving. If taking amounts to the same thing as giving, then by all good logic the reverse must also be true: giving amounts to the same thing as taking. It is true firstly because as Malinowski insists, the Kula is a ring and what the Trobrianders give, say, a necklace, will eventually find its way back to the point of departure. What they give they will take back, even if belatedly. Yet giving amounts to the same thing as taking for another, even more fundamental reason. The Kula is not merely a ring, but also a form of exchange, and what this means is that the Trobrianders will take *as* they give. Long before the necklace makes the round of the Kula, the gift has already gone round and come round in the form of the counter-gift – a bracelet – the circle of the gift has already completed itself. It always completes itself before it completes itself – in a little more than an instant, however small this 'little' might be. We shall discuss this instant, if it exists at all, in due course. Let us simply note here that another way of saying what we, and Malinowski, in his own way, have been saying is to argue that there is no such thing as gift, that what passes for a gift is simply another form of exchange. Malinowski does, in fact, say this, even if not in so many words. In the *Argonauts* he is still referring to pure gifts, as if there can be impure gifts and still be gifts. In *Crime and Custom*, however, he will reconsider his position. In the chapter 'The Principle of Give and Take Pervading Tribal Life', he will note that 'when ... I describe [in the *Argonauts*] a category of offerings as

"Pure Gifts" and place under this heading the gifts of husband to wife and of father to children, I am obviously committing a mistake'. The mistake, Malinowski goes on to say, was to take this transaction out of context and hence fail to see that it was part of a circle, a wider chain of transactions in which the presumed gift was in fact payment for services received. Malinowski will note further:

> In the same paragraph I have supplied, however, an implicit rectification of my mistake in stating that 'a gift given by the father to his son is said [by the natives] to be a repayment for the man's relationship to the mother' (p. 179). I have also pointed out there that the 'free gifts' to the wife are also based on the same idea (Malinowski 1926: 40).

It seems then, that nothing is *free* – and as we will see, no one is free either – not even the gifts that circulate in the household and sustain the relationship between spouses and between parents and children. Even such 'pure relationships' – to use an expression meant to apply to what is presumed to be a very different kind of society[2] – are not pure. They, too, are tainted by calculation, whether conscious or unconscious. If one takes – as one must – one gives, and if one gives, one takes, as in any other kind of economic transaction – barter, for example, or buying and selling. The household is itself an economy – *oikonomia* – the first one perhaps, and if the household is an economy, nothing else can escape the law of division, distribution, and exchange. To say this is not to deny the *phenomenon* of the gift, what passes as gift, the fact in other words that people exchange what they consider to be gifts. It is, rather, to highlight the fact that it is only a phenomenon or, what is another way of saying the same thing, that the gift itself or in itself whose phenomenon people deal with in everyday life is a phantom. Nor is this to deny the phenomenological difference between gift exchange and other forms of exchange. Apparently, unlike barter or buying and selling where exchange is immediate, the cycle of what passes as the gift takes time to complete itself. And it is true, too, that there is a tempo involved, a range of options as to the time delay between gift and counter-gift that, as Bourdieu (1977) says in his own discussion of the gift, is constitutive of the process and can be used strategically by the recipient to his or her advantage. Yet all this makes it no less a form of exchange and an economy than barter or buying and selling, despite the mystique with which it is usually surrounded.

The impossibility of the gift (and the preponderance of the economy), which we are noting here in a preliminary fashion and which we will discuss in all its complexity in the next chapter, is an important premise in its own right even if not a new one. But it is important also because of what it says – provided that one is prepared to listen carefully – about other, seemingly unrelated but significant issues, epistemological and political, which are themselves surrounded by a certain mystique. As in the case of the gift with which we are all familiar, the mystique has to do with the ability to give without taking beforehand, hence also without taking with the other hand, the one that does not do the giving. It has to do with the power of giving, as we will call it, the presumed ability to give beyond or outside every conceivable economy, which may be what ability or power ultimately mean – making something (a) present from nothing. There is much at stake in the demystification of this notion, first and foremost the status of the Western intellectual and cultural tradition, what I will call here European thought for short, which is premised on such a magical power. What is at stake to begin with is a certain intellectual gift, or gift of thought – not that it is ever conceptualised in such terms. Nonetheless, if one listens carefully to what the terms say, one would not fail to hear its name. The gift in question is what the subject takes *for granted*, namely, as the term itself suggests what it takes as a grant or gift. It should, of course, take nothing for granted – not a single thing. For European thought there is no gift of thought, if by gift we mean what one subject gives to another. This is a given (gift of thought). For European thought the subject ought to think for itself, give itself the gift of thought through its own devices – an auto-gift, we might say. This is also a given (gift of thought), and it is foundational. It is precisely what it means to be enlightened and the motto of the Enlightenment: think for yourself – which is what the enlightened subject takes for granted as a grant or gift.

At stake is also the gift that this presumed auto-gift of thought makes possible, if it does. Thinking for oneself may be 'the touchstone of truth', as Kant says, but it is far more than that. It is also the condition of possibility of auto-nomy – another auto-gift. For it should be clear that the subject that thinks for itself no longer depends on others for the truth. It produces or validates it – the two terms amount to the same thing in this context – all by itself. And because it no longer needs to take anything (for granted), it no longer needs to give anything either – neither to give in (to others) nor to give up (its independence). This, too, is foundational. It is, among other things, an essential ingredient of the distinction between the modern and the traditional – broadly speaking, the distinction between those who supposedly question and doubt everything and by doing so constitute themselves as autonomous subjectivities and those who conform by repeating what is handed down to them. What is at stake finally in this discussion of the impossibility of the gift is the gift of thought that those who give themselves the gift of thought – true knowledge and understanding – thereby giving themselves also the gift of autonomy give to the rest of the world. The story of *this* gift – the gift of European thought – is well known and need not detain us long. It is the story of the white man's burden, the task of civilising the world that this 'man' set for himself all by himself – for he thought and no doubt still thinks that he is capable of thinking for himself. This task proved to be a burden precisely because even though the white 'man' gave everything he had – light – he received nothing in return to make his labour in the tropics worthwhile, not even gratitude – which, let us hasten to add, is no longer the case, at least in certain postcolonial quarters, some more unlikely than others. As we will see in the next chapter, gratitude is now more forthcoming – *now* meaning the time after colonialism, the postcolonial era. Although European thought ought to be criticised, even provincialized or decentred, which is the task that postcolonial discourse sets itself – also all by itself because it, too, thinks that it thinks for itself – there is also recognition that this thought is a gift to us all and we should therefore be grateful for it. But what if there is no gift, as we have been saying – what if this gift of thought is nothing? Would not the gratitude we are expected to express be for nothing?

This is what this book is driving at, where it is slowly going. Its contention is that there is no auto-gift of thought, only the gift's suppressed other, an economy of thought where, as in every economy – for there are many – giving amounts to the same thing as taking and taking to the same thing as giving. I have just intimated that Kant, the pillar of the Enlightenment if ever there was one, was well aware of the existence of this economy even if apparently he did not call it by this name. He certainly knew very well that when it comes to the question of knowledge, giving is nothing more than taking and taking nothing more than giving. But he also believed that it was possible to break the circularity and step outside the circle. Hence the directive to take nothing for granted – for there is no such thing as a grant or gift of thought – encapsulated in the motto of the Enlightenment: think for yourself. Kant staked everything on this prospect and lost – instantly, at the very moment he defined what enlightenment meant. And so did all those who came after him, took up his directive, and sought to abide by it. Kant lost by virtue of giving; they lost by virtue of taking. If there is no gift of thought, there is no gift of thought, whether this gift is given by another person or by the self to itself – as an-auto gift, as we have just said. The subject always takes if it is to give anything at all and does so precisely because much like the Trobrianders who Malinowski paraded through the pages of the *Argonauts*, it is always dispossessed. Even when it takes nothing for granted, it always takes something for granted – as a bare minimum, the directive that it should take nothing for granted. Paradoxically, to think for itself the subject must not think for itself. This is to say that there is no free thinking or thinking for free, which should not be all that surprising, because as everyone knows nothing is free in the economy, there is always a cost of living to reckon with. If one takes – as one must – one gives. It is to say that here as elsewhere there is a price to pay for taking – a cost of thinking.

To schematise in the extreme and assert what will have to be demonstrated, for the epistemic subject the price to pay for taking is subjectivism, for the political subject subjection. The first cost is more familiar than the second. The subject is subjective not so much because it takes for granted at the discursive level as the philosophers of the Enlightenment assumed – an assumption that underscores also the Marxist notion of ideology. If that were the case, things would have been simpler. The subject is subjective rather primarily because, as it is often said in the literature, its vision of the world reflects its position in social space, its historical, social, and cultural conditioning, in short, because of what it has taken for granted to become what it is – a subject of one sort or another. And although what it is is a historical accident and not cast in stone – for it can no doubt change and eventually become something different – what it can never to do is be nothing, which is to say, objective. If it were possible for the subject to purge itself from everything it has taken for granted – which is not – it would no longer be subjective. But it would no longer be subject either. It would turn itself into an object – a thing. For the same reasons the subject is always already subject to the powers that be. To put it schematically once again, if to be subject rather than a thing the subject must take for granted, and if it acts on the basis of what it knows rather than out of pure impulse – for, as we shall see, in that case too it would not be subject – then it forecloses the possibility of ever becoming autonomous. Having taken for granted, it has already given in to the powers that be and given up this prospect. It always already gives in and gives up even when, at the limit, the only thing it ever needs to take for granted to become autonomous is the directive to take nothing for granted. This is to say that to be autonomous the subject must not be autonomous, that to criticise, resist, revolt against authority it must conform to it. Such is the paradox of living in what I have chosen to call political economy: political because it is about struggles, whether individual or collective, to liberate the self from the powers that be, and economy because here, too, there is a price to pay for taking, a cost of doing.

This brings me finally to European thought itself, its revolution – the intellectual and cultural movement known as the Enlightenment – and re-volution – what appears as the historical trajectory that brings back to the point of departure. If, as we have been saying, there are no auto-gifts of thought, hence no autonomy either, the conclusion that European thought has gone round and come round seems unavoidable. Much like the necklaces and bracelets of the Kula ring, it has come full circle: from the time when the individual was not thinking for itself and was therefore subject to the powers that be – the time before the Enlightenment – to the time when it finally dawned on the modernist subject that the individual cannot think for itself and is therefore beyond liberation – our time which, as we shall see, some chose to call, with good reason, postliberatory. I have been saying it *appears* and it *seems* because the circle that I am highlighting here has become visible only in recent decades – which is not to say that because it is now visible it is also accepted in its finality. Yet this circle has been there from the beginning for everyone to see, and some did in fact see it, however dimly. Once again, a comparison with the Kula ring may be instructive here. As I have already suggested, the Kula is a ring or a circle not only or even mainly because, as Malinowski argues, the objects exchanged always return to the point of departure. It is always already a circle – the circle of the gift. The gift/necklace comes back to the point of the departure before it comes back to the point of departure – in a little more than an instant – in the form of the counter-gift/bracelet. In much the same way, European thought has always already gone round and come round, at the moment of its conception or conceptualisation – on account, as we have said, of the giving that was also taking and the taking that was also giving (in and up).

All this suggests that there is really not very much to say about the question of European thought being a gift to the rest of the world, much less about the gratitude that the rest owes the West. In all seriousness we may ask: What gift? What European thought? All we have encountered at the foundations of this intellectual and cultural edifice is contradictions. And why should anyone expect that it would be otherwise? Is not 'the system at war with itself' (Douglas 1966: 140)? Surely, this was not meant only for the Mae Enga.[3]

* * * * *

At the time of writing these introductory lines I was staying in a friend's house for a few days. One morning as I was drinking coffee, I noticed on the mug I was holding the following inscription: 'Owned by no one. Free to challenge anything. The Guardian'. *The Guardian* is a well-known and respected British newspaper, and I was mildly amused to find out that the mug was given out free when one bought a copy of the paper. But the inscription also struck me because it confirmed yet again the strong hold or stronghold that the idea of autonomy has over the modernist imagination, the magical aura that surrounds this notion to the extent that it makes it suitable for a promotional ploy. It is true, no doubt, that if one is owned by no one, one is free. But is there such a subject? And if there is, would it have any reason to challenge anything when itself is challenged by nothing?

To suggest an answer to these questions in a more empirically grounded manner I will turn to an example from Mediterranean ethnography – Bourdieu's (1977) work on the Kabyle.[4] If the Kabyle man is challenged, says Bourdieu, the code of honour requires that as a general rule he responds with a counter-challenge. For what is at stake is his reputation as a man. But there are exceptions to this rule. When the challenge comes from a clearly inferior man, he can refuse to take it seriously without losing face. The challenge of the inferior man does not challenge him enough to take it up and respond with a counter-challenge. Perhaps it does not challenge him at all and leaves him completely indifferent. Whatever the case, the superior man does not take the challenge seriously and does not take it up. Being superior, he has no need to *take* – note that the challenge may well be a gift of some sort. At the limit, he is so superior that he depends on no one. He is therefore free. But precisely because he is free, he is not challenged by anything or anyone and has no need to challenge anything or anyone in turn. He is completely indifferent to the world. Such, as we shall see in due course, is what many have come to recognise as the sterility of freedom. There is no such man, of course – and this may be just as well. There is no such man not because there are no superiors and inferiors in the world but because for every superior there is someone else who is even more superior and someone else who is more superior still so that, to follow this logic to its logical conclusion (if it has one), it is superiors all the way up and no doubt inferiors all the way down.

It seems then, that to challenge anyone, to criticise, resist, rebel, or revolt against, or more simply engage with, the subject must itself be challengeable. Someone or something must have a certain hold over it. The subject, in short, must not be free. This is also how this book is implicated in what it says about European thought and its presumed gift – autonomy. It is yet another proof, if another proof is needed, that there is no such thing.

Notes

1. I have called this elsewhere the salvation intent (Argyrou 2002).
2. Modern societies, according to Giddens (1991).
3. 'Perhaps all social systems are built on contradiction, in some sense at war with themselves' (Douglas 1966: 140).
4. But see also Herzfeld's (1985) work on the island of Crete.

CHAPTER 2

THE GIFT OF EUROPEAN THOUGHT

The Postcolonial

As I hope is obvious from has been said, provincializing Europe cannot ever be a project of shunning European thought. For at the end of European imperialism, European thought is a gift to us all. We can talk of provincializing it only in an anticolonial spirit of gratitude (Chakrabarty 2000: 255)

This quotation is from a book that belongs to the genre of postcolonial theory or, better still, postcolonial critique, since critique is the avowed intention and rationale of this theory – in theory at least. It is the last paragraph of the book, and it makes a final attempt to manage the deep-seated contradiction that haunts the book but also, more broadly, the genre to which the book belongs. Yet the contradiction proves intractable, and the fragments of the text spill over into the margins and beyond the book itself. Let us name this contradiction before proceeding any further. And let us do so by using an imaginative expression from another postcolonial critic, even if her intention was not necessarily to name the contradiction as such. 'One of the things … I believe one must do is the persistent critique of what you cannot not want' (Spivak (1991: 39). To criticise what one desires and to do so persistently – such is the impossible task that the postcolonial critic sets herself.

I should say, to place the statement in context, that Spivak is commenting on the observation that she achieved much of what she had set out to achieve – among other things, her interviewer points out, 'the establishment of a recognition in first-world feminism of the limits of its claim to establish universalizing norms for women in general' (1991: 38). But she does not agree with this evaluation: 'It is very kind of you [the interviewer] to say that these things have already been achieved – I must say it doesn't look like that to me' (1991: 39). Her response may be more than just an expression of undue modesty. It may well be the case that the postcolonial critic is pointing to a real problem, a paradox where the things that have been achieved – '[T]hey're on the agenda!' (1991: 39), exclaims the interviewer, as if this explains everything and settles everything – have not been achieved. One cannot not want these things to be on the agenda. This is precisely what one has been striving for all along. But having placed them there, one discovers that this is not what one wants either, that it is and it is not at the same time. It is what one wants because first-world feminism now recognises the limits of its own discourse and does not set universalising norms for third-world women delegating them in this way to an inferior position. But it is not what one wants because, it seems, third-world women still emerge as inferior in the discourse of first-world feminism even as it meticulously refrains from setting universalising standards. It seems that the more one talks about them the more likely it is that they would be cast as inferior. It is as if discourse unfolds on the basis of its own independent logic and cannot be made to say what one wishes it to say no matter how hard one tries. It is as if the mere act of representing these women is also an act of making them different – for how else can one begin even to think about another if that other is not other but the same? – as if the moment of encountering them as themselves is deferred or postponed indefinitely, which is not to say that these women or anyone else for that matter ever encounter and know themselves as themselves. As we shall see in our discussion of time, there is no such moment. The moment of encounter is either always in the future and has not arrived yet or has always already arrived and is in the past. It seems, in short, that the process of othering is out of everyone's control.[1]

To take Spivak's statement out of context then, but only slightly, postcolonial discourse is the persistent critique of what one desires. What one wants, or more tellingly, what one should not want but cannot stop wanting it no matter how hard one tries – the gift that European thought is said to be in the quotation above – is also what one must criticise and do so persistently. European thought is at once an object of critique and an object of desire. It is the status of this object, if that is what it is, that makes postcolonial discourse unstable and contradictory. If European thought is a gift, if it is recognised and has been accepted as such, it cannot be an object of critique. If it is not a gift but an insult, an othering of one sort or another, a gift of poison,[2] it cannot be an object of desire. Something has to give – desire for the sake of critique or critique for the sake of desire. Yet nothing does. Postcolonial discourse is unable to decide what this object is hence unable to decide also what it itself must be to deal with it. It is at once positive and critical; it celebrates European thought as a gift but also rejects it as an insult. Such is the contradiction. Postcolonial discourse strives to be both and ends up being neither: neither the one nor the other; neither here nor there. Yet this does not make it a liminal entity, at least not in the proper anthropological sense of the term. Although 'between and betwixt' being a critique and a celebration of

European thought, unlike other entities in a liminal state, postcolonial discourse is permanently caught up in it. It has nowhere to go, no set trajectory and no destination. Desire cannot be sacrificed for the sake of critique but neither can critique be silenced for the sake of desire. The two seem to have been locked in a fateful embrace and cannot be apart. And they seem to have been locked in this way from the very beginning.

'One is *tempted* to say', says Zizek (2000: 255; my emphasis) in a related context, 'that the will to gain political independence from the colonizer in the guise of a new independent nation-state is the ultimate proof that the colonized ethnic group is thoroughly integrated into the ideological universe of the colonizer'. Let us note here in passing – not because it is a trivial matter but because I will return to it – that Zizek is *tempted* to say this. He is saying it, but he is not certain that he should be saying it or whether he means what he says. Despite the hesitation, the implication of what he says (without really saying it) should be clear. Without the desire to become like the coloniser – an independent nation-state with everything else that this implies – there would be no grounds for criticising colonialism as a form of political domination much less for rebelling against it.[3] Desire is the condition of possibility of critique and, reciprocally, critique is a manifestation or symptom of desire. The two sustain each other in a circular relationship and cannot exist independently of one another. If such is the case however, postcolonial discourse is destined to remain a liminal entity circulating from critique to desire and back without ever becoming either the one or the other. It is destined to remain contradictory and inarticulate, unable to say what it is and what it does exactly.

This theme of desire for the object of critique or critique of the object of desire is endlessly enacted in colonial and postcolonial discourse, but here I will briefly mention only two paradigmatic examples. I have chosen them precisely because, put together, they sketch the image of the persona at the centre of this drama, hence, also what it is about European thought that is both desired and critiqued. The first example – 'a heritage of all postcolonial thinkers', says Chakrabarty (2000: 5) – is Fanon's (1967) attempt to hold on to the 'man' discovered by European 'man' but betrayed by him in practice – notably if not exclusively, as Fanon himself says, through the violence of colonialism. The second example is Spivak's desire to hold on to the 'woman' discovered by European 'woman' but also betrayed by her in practice – not necessarily because of any intention to betray her, as we have just noted. This 'man' and this 'woman' then, put together, illustrate what it is about the object of critique that is desired. It is inclusion in the species invented by European thought, the secular, abstract, and universal human – abstract and universal but with particular attributes, most notably and fundamentally, autonomy. It also illustrates what it is about the object of desire that must be criticised – Europe's failure to uphold the ideal that it itself produced. Although posited in theory, this species of the human has been endlessly betrayed in practice. Although conceived by and nurtured in the European imagination, Europe has never been able to give birth to it in society and history. Hence, the urgent and serious task that (post)colonial discourse sets itself: to expose the limits of European thought and find ways to transcend them, to make theory practice, imagination living reality. It wishes to do so as though the limits of thought were specifically European, as though Europe would not have transcended them if anything of the sort were ever possible. 'Let us decide not to imitate Europe [imitate it, that is, in its failure to practice what it preached].... Let us try to create the whole man, whom Europe has been incapable of bringing to triumphant birth' (Fanon 1967: 252). Europe conceived the 'man' that the other 'man' so much desires. The (post)colonial critic will deliver and raise him.

Having highlighted the contradiction that haunts postcolonial discourse in general, we can now return to the specific example with which we began. It should be clear even from a casual reading that what is at stake in this quotation is the meaning of the phrase 'provincializing Europe' – which is also the title of the book – and how to manage it. The postcolonial critic hopes that the meaning of this phrase would be obvious from what the book has been saying before reaching the end. Yet the nagging suspicion persists that it may not be so obvious after all. And it persists with good reason. For what the book has been saying reflects precisely the contradiction we have located and can be read both as rejection and celebration of European thought. Because the text lacks the conceptual clarity it pretends to have, the postcolonial critic feels the need to make a final attempt to set the record straight. He feels the need to specify the correct reading and clarify the intended message of the book – for the sake of the truth no doubt and the sake of the (European) reader as well, but not only. The postcolonial critic feels the need to clarify things in his own mind as well, for his benefit and his own sake. For as we shall see shortly, what is at stake in the 'proper' reading of the text is also, over and above anything else, the postcolonial critic's own existence. This final paragraph, then, attempts to reassure the (European) reader as much as the postcolonial critic himself that provincializing Europe does not mean what it could be reasonably taken to mean, what the idea of turning Europe into a province itself points to: dislodging it from the centre, pushing it into the corner or the margins, demonstrating that it is only one province in the world among many others, not worse perhaps, certainly not better than other provinces. Such would be the aim of a culturally relativist discourse, and by its own admission this is not such a project: 'The project of provincializing Europe ... cannot be a project of cultural relativism' (Chakrabarty 2000: 41). It cannot ever be such a project, says the postcolonial critic speaking for us all, because European thought is a gift to us all (presumably non-Europeans), and as everyone knows, a gift cannot be rejected lightly. The rules of reciprocity forbid it. If there is an obligation to give – in this case the obligation known as the white man's burden – there is also an obligation to receive and an obligation to give something back even if nothing more than a symbolic equivalent, such as the expression of gratitude. This is what this last paragraph does – on the face of it, at one level of analysis. It gives back to Europe and gives the cycle of reciprocity and complicity between Europe and non-Europe the push that keeps it turning.

As we have noted, the *obligation* to give back to Europe – which already suggests that the gift of European thought has been transmuted into a *debt* to be repaid and is no longer gift (if it has ever been) – is also an obligation to oneself. The postcolonial critic owes it to himself to affirm that European thought is a gift and express gratitude. For this gift has already been received, kept, appropriated, become one's own property as the proper thing to have and to be. European thought is no longer the thought of Europeans only. It is also, and as much, the postcolonial critic's thought. How, then, can he not not want it? In wanting it, the postcolonial critic wants nothing more or less than himself. How can he not not affirm that this thought is a gift? In doing so, the critic also affirms the value of his own subjectivity. To dislodge Europe from the centre, to force it into the corner or the margins, as the neologism *provincializing* suggests, is not an option and must be rejected. It would be tantamount to decentring and marginalising oneself. The postcolonial critic may be persistent in his critique of European thought, but persistence has limits. Chakrabarty is well aware of this. As he points out early on in the book, '*relating* to a body of thought to which one largely owes one's intellectual existence cannot be a matter of exacting … "postcolonial revenge"' (2000: 16; my emphasis).[4] It cannot be such a matter because it would mean retaliating not only against Europe but also against oneself. Not that this sort of self-punishment is unheard of, of course, but neither is it what people do as a matter of course. The need to preserve oneself at the centre, maintain a centre, and be what one is (if such control was ever possible) prevails and sets limits to how critical the postcolonial critic can be. As Butler (1997: 129) recognises in another structurally similar context, the desire to be what one is (or what one thinks that one is) 'at once conditions and limits the viability of … critical interrogation.… One cannot criticize too far the terms by which one's existence is secured'.

There is more to this structure than meets the eye. If too much criticism is threatening, so is too little. Below a certain threshold the critique is no longer viable as critique. It becomes a matter of simply 'relating' to European thought, a term that I highlighted in the quotation above because it is symptomatic of the ill-fated attempt to manage the meaning of provincialization. Yet if the critique is no longer viable, if it simply masquerades as critique, neither is the postcolonial critic's identity as a postcolonial critic. This identity goes by the board. But what of a critique that criticises neither too much nor too little? Is it not possible to strike a balance, find the right measure, construct a critique that would be viable without at the same time undermining the critic's modernist identity? There is no such critique. If it is viable, it is undermining; if it is not viable, it is also undermining. It the first case it undermines the postcolonial critic as a modernist subjectivity, in the second, the modernist subjectivity as a postcolonial critic. I have suggested above that postcolonial discourse is destined to circulate from critique to desire and back without ever becoming either the one or the other. Much the same can be said about the subject that produces it. It too is destined to remain inarticulate oscillating between a modernist identity and the identity of a postcolonial critic, criticising European thought here and praising it as a gift there or, more embarrassingly, doing both at the same time in the narrow confines of the same short paragraph.

If provicializing Europe cannot be a matter of rejecting European thought and exacting postcolonial revenge, as the postcolonial critics says, neither can it be a matter of simply relating to it. The postcolonial critic knows this, of course. He knows it well and must find space in this short paragraph at the end of the book to make a statement to this effect, even if such a statement will contradict what he has said in the preceding two sentences. Having clarified the meaning of provincialization in a way that it is not misconstrued as negation of European thought, having made certain that it does not acquire a life of its own as critique and does not come back seeking postcolonial revenge – a case of preventing 'semantic fetishism', one might say – the critic must now introduce another clarification, a clarification of the clarification. He must ensure that he has not gone too far to the other side, given away too much, given in to the opposition, generated the impression that his discourse is nothing more than a neutral, disinterested discussion of European thought. He must, in short, say something in the last sentence to remind the (European) reader and no doubt himself that there is something wrong with the gift of European thought. Having given with one hand, the postcolonial critic is about to take with the other.

Let us follow the steps that he takes in this taking, which is not to say that he is taking all the steps consciously or is in control of the text. As we have said, in the first and second sentence of the paragraph the postcolonial critic assures the reader and himself that provincialization does not mean negation of European thought. In the final sentence however, there is a pronounced shift in attitude and the reader is left wondering whether the author meant what he said in the first two sentences: 'We can talk of provincializing it [European thought] only in an anticolonial spirit of gratitude' (Chakrabarty 2000: 255). What generates uncertainty in this last sentence is the term *anticolonial*. The postcolonial critic is grateful for the gift he says European thought is but in a way that is inconsistent with the expression of gratitude – *anti*. Before I explore this point further, however, it is necessary to note that there is another shift in this last sentence, more subtle but as important – a shift in the semantic content of the term *provincializing*. A close reading of the paragraph suggests that the meaning of provincialization in the last sentence is not the same as the meaning of provinicialization in the first. It is the reverse. If it were the same, the last sentence would make little sense. It would read as saying something along the following lines: 'We can talk of accepting European thought as a gift only in a spirit of gratitude.' There is something fundamentally dissonant about this. There is, to begin with, the implication, encapsulated in the terms *can* and *only*, that in talking about accepting a gift one is taking liberties. One *can* talk about it *only* under specific conditions, namely, in a spirit of gratitude. Without this spirit one presumably would not take the liberty of talking about it in this way – as a gift to be accepted. Secondly, the sentence is redundant. There is no other way of accepting a gift except by expressing gratitude. If there is no gratitude, there is no gift. The gift or, at any rate, what passes as gift, becomes a payment, something considered due and repaid.

A more reasonable reading would be the following: 'We can talk of *rejecting* European thought only in a spirit of gratitude.' This reading explains why one may be taking liberties in talking this way. One can take liberties and use the language of rejection because given the circumstances specified by the term *only*, it should be clear to the reader that this is just talk, that rejection of European thought is symbolic, not real. It should be clear, in other words, that the postcolonial critic does not mean what he says – which is not to say that he necessarily meant not to mean what he says. It may well be the case that he is guided by his discourse rather than guiding it, that the shift in the semantic content of the term *provincialization* was unintentional, even though it no doubt is revealing.

Let us finally turn to the term we have bracketed off. The postcolonial critic gives thanks for the gift he has taken from Europe in an anticolonial spirit. He is grateful for this gift but expresses his gratitude with an attitude – defiantly, in the spirit of opposition or resistance – in short, in a way that gratitude cannot be expressed if it is to remain gratitude. The postcolonial critic seems to mean what he says here, but does what he says mean anything? Read out of content it does not amount to much. He is contradicting himself by denying in advance what he is about to assert – gratitude. Read in context, he is still contradicting himself, but it is now easier to see that there is method in this madness. The contradiction is not gratuitous. It is the inevitable outcome of the postcolonial condition. The postcolonial critic must attempt to salvage whatever is left of the critical edge of the discourse and of his own identity as a postcolonial critic before the (European) reader closes and puts down the book. Before it is too late, before 'wrong' impressions are formed by everyone concerned, he must remind the (European) reader as much as himself that not all is well with European thought, that this gift is also an insult. He recalls therefore, perhaps even calls for the spirit of anticolonial resistance and struggle as if these were still colonial times, as if the independence that was granted – as a grant or gift no doubt – was denied as it was granted, at the same time. As we shall see, there is more substance to this hypothesis than meets the eye.

Provincializing Europe, as the exemplary form of postcolonial critique that it pretends to be, does not even consider the possibility that European thought may not be what it appears to be. It must be a gift – all signs to the contrary notwithstanding – if not for the sake of Europe that gave it (if it did), then for the sake of Europe's others or, at any rate, the sake of the postcolonial critic and other like-minded postcolonial subjectivities who took it and now cannot give it up, even if they have never had it and never will have it. For as we have already noted and will try to substantiate in what follows, there is nothing to have – no gift and no gift of thought, whether an auto-gift or one given by one subject to another. We have learnt from Derrida to treat the gift as a phantom, and we shall follow him in this discussion of European thought as a gift, at least part of the way. Before we turn to Derrida, however, let us return to the quotation with which we began, retrace our steps once again, and highlight what we have just announced – the signs of the impossibility of the gift and of European thought as gift. The key statement in this respect is the second sentence: 'At the *end* of European imperialism European thought is a gift to us all.' It should be clear that for the postcolonial critic European thought has not always been a gift. It may have been given as a gift from the beginning but it became gift only at the end – the 'end of European imperialism'. This claim raises a whole set of questions, including the metaphysical, quasi-religious question of the End, the plenitude associated with it, and whether there is an end to be reached or, as I have suggested in the first chapter of this book and will elaborate on in due course, a circle in which the end is also the beginning. For the moment, however, the question to be addressed is how something that was given as a gift – and we have the colonial civilising mission to vouch for this – was not a gift and did not become one until a specific time in the future – the end.

The answer to this question appears tantalisingly simple and eminently reasonable. The European coloniser of the nineteenth century, says the postcolonial critic by way of explanation, preached Enlightenment humanism at the colonised but denied it in practice. I shall take Enlightenment humanism – the vision of the abstract and universal human – as a shorthand designation of the European gift to the rest of the world, as this is the heading also under which the postcolonial critic himself subsumes a number of key concepts associated with European thought, culture and history:

> Concepts such as citizenship, the state, civil society, public sphere, human rights, equality before the law, the individual, distinctions between public and private, the idea of the subject, democracy, popular sovereignty, social justice, scientific rationality, and so on all bear the burden of European thought and history.... These concepts entail an unavoidable – and in a sense indispensible – *universal and secular vision of the human*. The European colonizer of the nineteenth century both preached this Enlightenment humanism at the colonized and at the same time denied it in practice (Chakrabarty 2000: 4; my emphases).

The gift of European thought then, was given to the colonised only in theory, which is to say, it was not given to them at all. It was promised but not actually delivered, postponed or deferred until the end, and one could reasonably say that during all this time, from the beginning to the end, it was nothing more than a gift in suspension, a virtual reality, a phenomenon, perhaps even a phantom. But there is a problem with this seemingly reasonable explanation. For although only a virtual reality, Enlightenment humanism affected the lives of the colonised of the nineteenth century in profound ways; although not actually given to them, they nonetheless actually took it and put it into (what they thought of as) good use. As the postcolonial critic himself points out, they 'embraced' and 'appropriated' it as the proper thing to have. But how can a gift that was never actually given nonetheless be taken? How can something that does not exist have real effects on the world? One could, of course, point out that there is nothing strange about this, that phantoms, or visions, or ideas affect the real world and do so all the time, as a matter of course. This is no doubt true, but to explain how something of this sort happens one needs to grant these phantoms some sort of reality, even if only subjective. In this particular case, one has to recognise that Enlightenment humanism was a gift to the colonised even if it was not given to them in practice. Yet the postcolonial critic is not prepared to accept such a phenomenological argument. It would undermine his argument and complicate his case enormously. He must therefore insist that Enlightenment humanism was nothing before the end of European imperialism, just an empty promise. He must insist because he believes in the objective reality of the gift, the possibility of the gift itself or, to use Kantian terminology, the gift in itself as opposed to its phenomenon. He must insist, in short, because he believes that the gift can be something other than an empty promise. This is to say that the postcolonial critic operates with a precritical understanding of the gift. And because he operates in this way, he is unable to explain how a phantom can be embraced and appropriated. It is worth quoting at some length here:

> The European colonizer of the nineteenth century both preached this Enlightenment humanism at the colonized and at the same time denied it in practice. But the *vision* has been powerful in its effects.... The modern Bengali educated middle classes ... have been characterised by Tapan Raychaudhuri as the 'the first Asian social group of any size whose mental world was transformed through its interaction with the West'. A long series of illustrious members of this social group – from Raja Rammohun Roy, sometimes called 'the father of modern India', to Manabendranath Roy, who argued with Lenin in the Comintern – warmly *embraced* the themes of rationalism, science, equality, and human rights that the European Enlightenment promulgated. Modern social critiques of caste, oppression of women, the lack of rights for laboring and subaltern classes in India, and so on – and, in fact, the very *critique of colonialism itself* [Zizek's and our own point] – are unthinkable except as a legacy, *partially*, of how Enlightenment Europe was *appropriated* in the subcontinent (Chakrabarty 2000: 4; my emphases).

I have highlighted the word *partially* because I wish to underscore what I have already indicated as the strategy of the postcolonial critic, the method in this madness, namely, giving with one hand and taking with the other – a fitting practice, no doubt, for as we shall see below this is also the structure of the gift. Although it was the European Enlightenment that actually transformed the mental world of the Bengali middle classes, it also was not. Although modern social critiques, including the critique of colonialism, are unthinkable without the legacy of European thought, on second thought, they are not unthinkable. They are *partially* unthinkable – a term that attempts to find the right measure, to strike the right balance between the thinkable and the unthinkable, dependence on European thought and independence from it, desire for this symbolic object and the imperative to criticise it at the same time. I have also highlighted the terms *vision*, *embraced*, and *appropriated* to underscore what I will argue has been from the beginning the nature of the exchange between Europe and non-Europe: spectral and phantasmagorical, which is not to say without real consequences. No doubt, what the colonised of the nineteenth century embraced and made their own property was not a gift but the phantom of the gift. Yet this is what anyone, anywhere, at any time will ever be able to appropriate. Contrary to what the postcolonial critic argues in the last paragraph of his book, even 'at the end of European imperialism' the gift that European thought is said to be is nowhere to be found. It simply is not (a) present.

Many people, including many Europeans, would no doubt dispute the postcolonial critic's claim that European imperialism has ended.[5] But perhaps this is a slip of the tongue and not what the postcolonial critic really meant to say. Perhaps what he meant to say was the end of *colonialism*, not imperialism. As we have just seen, for the postcolonial critic the European colonisers of the nineteenth century preached autonomy at the colonised but refused to grant it in practice. They argued that 'Indians or Africans were *not yet* civilized enough to rule themselves' (Chakrabarty 2000: 8). It would make sense therefore to say that European thought became a gift at the end of colonialism because it was only then that Indians and Africans were allowed to practice what it was preached to them. But even if this is what he meant to say, the claim that European thought is now a gift to us all is still untenable. Even at the end of colonialism, even more than half a century after the end, this gift has failed to materialise and is not (a) present. For if European thought were now a gift and not a phantom, why should anyone strive to provincialize Europe? Even if we accept that provincialization does not necessarily mean rejection or marginalisation, it is clear that something still must be done about or to Europe. But why, one might ask, if what it has done was to give non-Europe a gift? And why express gratitude for this gift in protest or resistance, in an anticolonial spirit? It may well be because the end of colonialism is not the end of colonialism, certainly not the end understood as the locus of plenitude – the site par excellence of autonomy.

To say that the end of colonialism is not the end of colonialism is not, of course, to say anything new. But it is to say it with a certain finality and at a level of generality that are perhaps not very common. For what we have been saying is that there is no end, that the end is also the beginning of another rotation of the circle. Be that as it may, a number of scholars have now come to recognise that colonialism was not only or even mainly direct political rule and oppression. It was also and more fundamentally a process of domestication, or colonisation, of the native mind (Comaroff and Comarof 1991), hence a matter of a more profound and long-lasting form of subjection than any sort of direct rule. As Asad (1991: 314) points out, the history of colonialism 'tells of European imperial dominance not as a temporary repression of subject populations but as an irrevocable process of transmutation, in which old desires and ways of life were destroyed and new ones took their place'. Although colonialism has apparently ended then, it has not ended. It continues to exist in the new desires and ways of life it produced, the new ways of thinking that it made impossible. The postcolonial subject is still dependent despite being independent – dependent on the powers that be for what it means to be – the gift of European thought still not a gift despite the fact that is being announced and celebrated as such. It is as if as soon as it appeared, it disappeared, and what remains of it is only a pale impression in the colonised and perhaps also the coloniser's imagination.

The postcolonial critic knows this too. He is well aware that even at the end of colonialism, even more than fifty years after the end the gift of European thought is nowhere to be found. He knows it and he wants us to know it as well from the outset, the very beginning of the book. If he claims otherwise at the end and contradicts himself, it is only because, for all the reasons we have already discussed, he cannot do otherwise. The problem after the end of colonialism then, the stumbling block that prevents the gift of European thought from becoming (a) present is historicism. This, the postcolonial critic explains, is a temporal structure which posits that everything of value – modernity, capitalism, the Enlightenment – takes place 'first in the West, then elsewhere' (2000: 6):

> Historicism is what made modernity or capitalism look not simply local but rather as something that became global *over time*, by originating in one place (Europe) and then spreading outside it. This 'first in Europe, then elsewhere' structure of global historical time was historicist. ... Historicism thus posited historical time as a measure of the cultural distance (at least in institutional development) that was assumed to exist between the West and the non-West. In the colonies, it legitimated the idea of civilization. In Europe itself, it made possible completely internalist histories ... in which Europe was described as the site of the first occurrence of capitalism, modernity, or Enlightenment (Chakrabarty 2000: 7).

What historicism does, then, is to deny precisely that which above anything else the postcolonial subject desires and depends on Europe to confirm, its being, as we have said: its being not in the past but in the present, not premodern and backward, not culturally inferior because different but on the contrary, and no doubt paradoxically, because of this very difference being of the same value and worth. But how can this be possible? Is it not the case that this sameness has been 'on the agenda' since the Enlightenment and the discovery of the secular, abstract, and universal human? And is it not true also that whenever it was removed from the agenda, or forgotten, or for some reason neglected, someone, whether from within or without Europe, always, sooner or later, put it back on the agenda and brought it to everyone's attention once again? Do we not live and have we not been living in an era in which this human is worshipped even as the only relevant god – an era not so secular after all – 'the cult of the individual', as Durkheim put it?[6] If so, how can historicism still exist and how can it be allowed to operate? As we shall see, the postcolonial critic will put it down to a bad habit of thought. But if so, this habit must be unshakable.

It is certainly the case that the historicist denial of cultural equality between Europe and non-Europe, what anthropologists have long identified as social evolutionism, need not be intentional to have effects. In a book title like *The Cultural Logic of Late Capitalism*, the postcolonial critic is quick to recognise the structure of historicism and hence an affirmation of Western superiority, even though the Western scholar who wrote the book may have been completely unaware that this is what his title entails and may have intended nothing of the sort. Indeed, it may even be the case that the intention of the book was precisely to criticise capitalism and modernity. Nonetheless, for the postcolonial critic '"late capitalism" is properly the name of a phenomenon that is understood as belonging primarily to the developed capitalist world, though its impact on the rest of globe is never denied'. In a similar vein, the historian who describes 'the coming of industries in England as the *first* industrial revolution' is guilty of historicism and ethnocentrism, even though it may be the case that as far as she is concerned, she was merely stating a historical fact (Chakrabarty 2000: 7). It is not so much that the postcolonial critic is wrong in his evaluation. What is leading him astray rather is the assumption that historicism – a manifestation of the temporalisation of time – can somehow be avoided.

We are then back to the question of a gift that is not what it appears to be, has not materialised, and is not (a) present despite the fact that it has long ceased being denied in practice and the fact that when it is denied in theory, it is often implicitly and unintentionally. We are back to this and the related question as to whether the gift of European thought will ever appear and be itself, which is also to ask whether there is an end to this journey or on the contrary, as we have argued, a circle on which the end is also the beginning. If history is anything to go by, one thing is certain: no one has ever seen the End (in all the senses of this term). The gift of European thought was given in theory during the colonial period, and although it was accepted by the colonised and put into practice, it was not a gift because the colonised were still subject to foreign rule. It was given in practice at the end of colonialism, but it is yet to materialise because in the postcolonial period it is denied in theory through historicism. And although this should not matter — for as the postcolonial critic argues it is practice that counts — it is clear that it does matter and matters enough to produce postcolonial critics and critiques. The question that remains to be considered is whether the postcolonial critic can himself or herself do something to secure this gift. If, as seems to be the case, it is impossible to give it — for giving it both in theory and practice have been tried and failed miserably — can it be obtained by other means? And if it is taken without having been given, would it still be gift? Postcolonial discourse is in a fundamental sense an attempt to take over the giving of this gift so that it can be given directly and without mediation by the self to itself, to make of this gift a gift to oneself — an auto-gift, as we have said. As the postcolonial critic himself phrases it, it is an attempt to renew European thought '*from* and *for*' the margins (Chakrabarty 2000: 16; my emphases):

> To critique historicism in all its varieties is to unlearn to think of history as a developmental process in which that which is possible becomes actual by tending to a future that is singular. Or, to put it differently, it is to learn to think the present — *the 'now' that we inhabit as we speak — as irreducibly not-one* [my emphasis]. To take that step is to rethink the problem of historical time and to review the relationship between the possible and the actual. The following thoughts derive from the discussion presented in the second division of Martin Heidegger's *Being and Time* (Chakrabarty 2000: 249).

The postcolonial critic is not far off the mark in singling out historicism as that which is in the way of the gift. Time as the present — whether the present now, the past present, or the future present — is of the essence of the gift, and it is no accident perhaps that, as I have intimated several time already, in everyday language the gift is also a present. Time is also the present as the gift and the fundamental question is whether they/it exist(s) at all and if so in what sense — the very question that Derrida raises and which we will discussed in the next section of this chapter. For the postcolonial critic by contrast this question does not even arise. The problem with historicism is not that it posits time as being (a) present — a now — but rather that it monopolises it. As far as European historicist thinking is concerned, there is only one present/gift, that of European modernity. Everything else is in its past. It is indicative of the postcolonial critic's faith in the possibility of the present/gift and indicative of his desire for the present/gift of European modernity, that he considers historicist thinking as one among other 'everyday habits of thought' (2000: 4). And he purports to explain how this habit can be broken and how proper thinking can be restored. But as soon as he begins to explain — in fact, even before he begins — he himself denies the possibility of breaking it. Before he even begins, he reproduces it.

To see this let us remind ourselves that the postcolonial critic's aim is to renew European thought 'from and for the margins'. Yet the question is this: renew it on the basis of what? Is the postcolonial critic purporting to introduce into European thought something new from the outside? It does not seem so. As he himself says, he derives the new in the renew, not from the margins but the centre – the work of Martin Heidegger. No doubt, Heidegger's work is different from the work of other European thinkers – Marx, for example. The work of the former, says the postcolonial critic, is 'hermeneutic', that of the latter 'analytical' (Chakrabarty 2000: 18). Yet as the appellation *hermeneutic* shows, there is no doubt either that it, too, belongs to the European intellectual tradition and is part of European thought. In fact, the issue here is not so much whether it belongs to it in the sense of having originated in Europe – Heidegger has often been accused of mysticism, which for his critics at least links him to the East. The issue rather is whether Europe authorises it – and this is precisely what it does by calling it hermeneutic, phenomenological, or existential. To be renewed from the margins then, European thought must first pass through the centre. It must *first* return to its source, the source of all legitimate signification – 'first in Europe' – and it is only then that it can begin the circular journey that will take it back to the margins once again – 'then elsewhere'. The postcolonial critic reproduces historicism even before he begins to explain to the rest of us how it can be eliminated. This is to say also that the attempt to renew European thought *'for* the margins', that is, to take over the giving of this gift for the benefit of the postcolonial subject, fails as well. This gift (if it exists) and its giving (if it is possible at all) remain firmly in the hands of those who monopolise it.

To round up the discussion I shall explore briefly the postcolonial critic's argumentation with regard to how the everyday habit of thought that historicism is said to be can be broken. Heidegger's thought, the postcolonial critic says, suggests that 'the now that we inhabit as we speak' is irreducibly not one; it is many. As I have already pointed out, the fundamental question is whether we do inhabit a 'now as we speak', whether there is a 'now' to inhabit, let alone many. Here, however, I will go along with claim of multiple presents and multiple modernities –because this is what the argument boils down to – to highlight the contradiction involved. The single now that historicism posits to the exclusion of everything else is, of course, the presence of modernity. On the basis of this presence, historicist thinking defines other ways of life, such as political modernity in India, as not being present, as the premodern past or, as we have seen in the case of the expression, late capitalism, as an early form of capitalism, hence still in the European past. The point of the postcolonial critic is that this imputed temporal absence of non-Europe is false. People in India and other parts of the world are contemporaries of Europeans. They may not live in the here of Europe, even though nowadays many do, but they certainly live in the same now as Europeans. They are 'coeval' to Europeans, as Fabian (1983) says in his own discussion of the same issue, whom the postcolonial critic quotes approvingly. Yet, as we have seen, the postcolonial critic's point is *also* that this present that 'we inhabit as we speak' and hence share is *'irreducibly* not-one'. It is more than one, all European attempts to reduce it to one in the guise of modernity notwithstanding. It is, therefore, both one and not one, a present that we all share as contemporaries but a present also that we do not share even though we are contemporaries. The postcolonial critic struggles with this contradiction. He desires the presence of modernity and modernity as a present but cannot accept the rejection of the presence of nonmodernity and *its* present. He struggles with it, but he can do no more than to reproduce it.

The presence of Europe's others, the postcolonial critic says, must not be conceptualised as incomplete or unrealised. That would be a historicist way of thinking about them, a way of saying that they are in Europe's past. The fundamental question, we have said, the question of all questions perhaps, is whether they or anyone or anything else for that matter, can be said to be present, whether the present itself as the now that we are supposed to inhabit as we speak exists at all. The postcolonial critic thinks that it does exist and that an alternative conceptualisation of Europe's others is therefore possible. He reasons as follows: 'For a possibility to be neither that which is waiting to become actual nor that which is merely incomplete, the possibility has to be thought of as that which already actually *is* but is present only as the "not yet" of the actual' (Chakrabarty 2000: 250). The sentence is no doubt painfully laboured, but does it mean anything? Perhaps it does even if not necessarily what the postcolonial critic would like it to mean. It is clear that what the postcolonial critic would like to say is something that reverses historicist thinking, something that shows that non-European cultures are not in the past of European modernity. They already actually *are*, he says; they exist and are present in the present. Yet there is an immediate qualification to this assertion. They exist and are present in the present *only* as – only as something that has not happened yet ('the not yet of the actual'), therefore, as something that is not present, even if, as the postcolonial critic insists, it is actual. On the basis of this logic then, Europe's others are both present and not present, both actual and virtual, here but also there, complete but also incomplete. What the postcolonial critic does here is what he has been doing elsewhere in the book, what he cannot avoid doing no matter how hard he tries – assert that something is and is not at the same time – contradict himself once again.

Any way one looks at it then, any way one – anyone – tries to make it appear in the light of day, the gift of European thought refuses to become (a) present. Those presumed to have it are unable to give it, even as they have given it both in theory and in practice – which raises the suspicion that they may have nothing to give. Those who do not have it can no more take it than take over its giving. Every time they try to do so, they run into intractable contradictions and paradoxes. The gift of European thought remains hidden in the shadows, cloaked in mystery, a spectre that haunts everyone that crosses its path, no one more so than the postcolonial subject. For it cannot not want it, as we have seen. More than two centuries of giving and taking both in theory and in practice, of being generous at one end and grateful at the other, of doing everything that needs to be done the way that it should be done, neither the European nor the postcolonial subject have anything to show for themselves. The gift of European thought is nowhere to be seen and no one can account for it, least of all those who proclaim so simply and effortlessly its existence in the end and at the end (of a book and a historical period). There may be a good reason for all this mystery. It may be the case that, as Derrida argues, the gift is impossible or even *the* impossible.

The Take on/of the Gift

Derrida begins his discussion of the impossibility of the gift with a reference to time, 'the time of the king', he who takes all of his 'morganatic' wife's time so that she has nothing left to give to anyone else. 'The King takes all my time', says the wife. 'I give the rest to Saint-Cyr, to whom I would like to give all' (Derrida 1994: 1). Derrida is reading from a letter by the king's wife that links in this way time and the gift – time as gift. Beginning the discussion by highlighting this link is not accidental. For Derrida time is of the essence of the gift. As I have already noted, time as the present – whether the present now, this instant, the past present, or future present – refers also to the presence of the gift and to the gift as a present.

The purpose of Derrida's preamble is to begin the process of problematizing the common sense understanding of time, hence that of the gift as well. He wants to question the assumption that time is some-thing, an entity of one sort or another that one can possess and therefore give, take, keep, set aside, waste, lose, or whatever else people in everyday life say they do with time. Derrida's argument is that in all such cases it is not time itself that one is dealing with. The word *time*, he says, refers metonymically to, or operates as another name for the things done *in* time or in the meantime, the things, in other words, that fill up the space which the absence of time itself opens up. Time itself does not belong to anyone, and hence, 'one can no more *take* it, itself, than *give* it'. For Derrida – who places himself with this argument in a long tradition of thinkers that stretches from Aristotle, to Saint Augustine, to Kant and Heidegger – time cannot belong to anyone because it does not exist. It is not anything. And because it does not exist, it can neither be given nor taken (lost, gained, wasted, set aside, and so on). In giving and taking time, one gives and takes nothing. This is to say, as Derrida says, that time 'undoes th[e] distinction between taking and giving, therefore also between receiving and giving, perhaps between receptivity and activity, or even the being-affected and the affecting of any affection' (Derrida 1994: 3).

I will deal with the collapse of the distinction between giving and taking in detail below – a collapse that, as we have seen, was in a certain sense anticipated by Malinowski in his discussion of the Kula. Here I wish simply to highlight and comment briefly on the undoing of the other distinction that Derrida refers to – that between receptivity and activity – as a way of anticipating the discussion that follows in subsequent chapters. The significance of this distinction can only become apparent if we substitute receptivity with passivity, the term against which activity is usually pitted. It is the distinction between the active and the passive, the production and reproduction, that carries the semantic load which make activity and production the privileged terms. If what Derrida has to say about time is anything to go by, however, there is no privilege to speak of. Let us first turn to the question of passivity. It should be clear that there can be no such thing as an inert subject for the simple reason that such a being would not be a subject but an object, a thing. Receptivity is a form of activity, much the same way that, as we shall see in the last chapter, taking for granted presupposes judgment, a decision to trust someone, hence also thinking for oneself. As for activity, there are problems here as well. To catch a glimpse of these problems we need to strain our ears to hear what the term says – from the Latin *actus*, meaning a doing, drive, urge, impulse. There can be no human acts that are the outcome of blind drives and impulses – blind because they do not see where they are coming from (as there is nothing to see), hence not where they are going either. Every doing, if it is human, presupposes thinking, however rudimentary it might be. It suffices that time temporalizes itself, that it becomes something more than an instant for thinking to occur. Even the most blind drive, the total loss of control which, let us say, leads to murder is not completely blind. The law recognises this. Even in such cases, it recognises the existence of *mens rea* or state of mind and holds the individual responsible, although it does distinguish between manslaughter and premeditated murder.

The issue with activity as opposed to receptivity-understood-as-passivity is not, of course, related to blind drives and impulses. However, the impossibility of human action said to be the outcome of such drives may help us to see the impossibility of human action to what activity is related, namely: originality, thinking for oneself, doing without having to take beforehand – for originality means precisely that there is no before – in short, making something (a) present from nothing. Let us note here that the plural of the Latin term *actus* is *agere*, from the Greek *agein*, to lead, drive, guide and related to *agent* in English and other European languages and of course *agency*. What survives for us in the 'active' is the doing, but as the other cognate terms suggest, this is not just any doing. There is something of the spontaneous and instantaneous about it, something unpredictable and uncontrollable, a doing that simply erupts on the scene as if it depends on nothing, comes from nowhere in particular and takes everyone by surprise. We can hear something of this sort in the terms *agent* and *agency*, particularly as these are used in the context of the structure and agency debate. To put it schematically, for those who take the latter point of view an agent is not a subject because it is not subject to the structures that structure the world. On the contrary, it is it that produces these structures – but on the basis of what? – and puts them in place to begin with; or, in a milder version of the same argument, if it is subject to them it nonetheless maintains a certain degree of freedom, a will of its own that is not reducible to any structure and which it can exercise at any time. If, however, there is no time, no present, now, this instant, there can be no agency in this sense, no instantaneous and spontaneous acts, no epiphanies, a deus ex machina. The distinction between receptivity and activity, passivity and activity collapses.

There are several themes that insinuate themselves here – the question of creativity and originality as in the distinction between arts and crafts, for example – but in the chapters that follow, I will examine only two permutations of this theme. The first is the theme of resistance to power and the question we will be asking is whether, paradoxically, it does not presuppose consent. The second is the distinction between the modern and the traditional that is itself predicated on the distinction between activity and passivity, the production of the new and the (mechanical) reproduction the old respectively.

But to return to the discussion of the gift, a few pages after the preliminary remarks on time Derrida will declare that 'wherever there is time, wherever time predominates or conditions experience in general ... the gift is impossible' (1994: 9). In fact, he has already announced that the gift is not simply impossible 'but *the* impossible. The very figure of the impossible. It announces itself, gives itself to be thought as the impossible' (1994: 7) – the emphasis on the *the* being Derrida's own. If anything can be said to personify the impossible, this is the gift. And it is impossible, Derrida says, or the impossible wherever *'there is'* time, wherever time conditions experience, which is to say, everywhere and at all times. Before I turn to the analytical steps that Derrida takes to substantiate his argument, it is necessary to discuss an apparent contradiction. On the one hand, Derrida claims that time does not exist and that what we are dealing with when we speak of it is not time itself but things done *in* time or in the meantime. On the other, he argues that 'there is' time and that it is precisely because of this that the gift is impossible. Derrida broaches this issue in the first pages of the book by drawing attention to the paradox in what the king's morganatic wife says. Although the king takes *all* her time, she still has some left, 'the rest', which she gives to Saint-Cyr (a charitable institution). But how can this be possible? If the king takes everything, *all* her time, it stands to reason that she should have no time left for anything else. Common sense suggests that the rest ought to be nothing. And so it is in a certain sense. Derrida's point is that the rest of time, what remains but logically should not, what she does not have but nonetheless gives, refers to time itself. It is a remainder because it always remains to be given and taken, no matter how much one gives or takes in time, even when what is given and taken is all of one's time. It always remains to be given because no one has it to give to anyone else. Time itself does not exist, as we have said. Yet 'it is not nothing', says Derrida, 'since it is beyond everything' or if it is nothing, nonetheless '*there is* [time] since she [the king's wife] *gives it*' (1994: 3).

How then, is the locution 'there is' to be understood? As Derrida himself points out, it is a Heideggerian expression used in the critique of the determination of the meaning of Being in Western metaphysics as presence. In this determination, to exist means to be present in the here and now or, at least, as Kant himself pointed out before both, to be an object of possible experience. For Heidegger however, (as much as for Derrida) time is not a temporal thing. It itself is not present, has never been present, and perhaps (for Heidegger) or unquestionably (for Derrida) will never be present in the empirical world. Although it conditions all experience, it itself cannot be experienced. Strictly speaking, therefore, one cannot say that 'time is' or 'Being is' because neither the one nor the other exists as an empirical reality. Nonetheless, we still think and talk about Being and time. Indeed, not only do we think and talk about them, but we also have a certain preconceptual understanding of them. Every time we use the word *is*, says Heidegger, we name Being. 'In every expressing of a proposition, e.g. "today is a holiday", we understand the "is", and equally what Being is,' Yet we do not know what it is. 'We thus understand Being, and yet we lack the concept. For all its constancy and breadth, this pre-conceptual understanding of Being is for the most part completely indeterminate' (Heidegger 1997: 159). Derrida makes a similar case about the gift. We precomprehend it, he says. We understand what it is but because we cannot experience it, we do not really know what it is. If we are to avoid the mistake committed by Western metaphysics then, that is, of thinking and talking about Being and time as if they were real entities, a different set of expressions must be used to denote them. Heidegger and Derrida after him use the expressions 'there is time' and 'there is being', which, as Derrida explains, in the original German, *es gibt*, also indicate giving – 'it gives time' and 'it gives being'. The 'enigma', says Derrida, 'is concentrated both in the "it" ... which is not a thing, and in this giving that gives but without giving anything and without anyone giving anything – nothing but Being and time (which are nothing)' (1994: 20).

There is, then, a contradiction in saying that Being and time are nothing and not nothing, but it is surmountable. At least this is what Kant taught, whom Heidegger and Derrida follow closely here. Very briefly and to use one of Kant's examples that is of particular interests to us in this discussion, one could say that the human being is both free and not free without necessarily contradicting oneself. The condition is that the human being is understood in a doubt sense – as a being in itself and as a phenomenon. In the former sense, the human being is free, in the latter it is subject to causation and hence not free.[7] This distinction will prove significant when we turn to discuss identity politics and the contradictions in which it is enmeshed. We shall argue that the only way to avoid these contradictions is to recognise that the autonomous individual is a figment of the imagination.

It may be pertinent to point out here also that linking Heidegger and Derrida to Kant, as I have done above, is not without strategic significance. My concern is to show that although Derrida (and no doubt Heidegger) is often cast as an enemy on the Enlightenment, he is deeply indebted to it. More specifically, my contention as it will unfold in the next chapter will be that the way to Derrida's critique of the (pure) gift has been paved by the Enlightenment, particularly Kant's critique of pure reason. This, of course, is not to say that Derrida is Kantian or that there are no differences between them. It is to say rather what Derrida himself acknowledges: that although 'the effort of thinking or rethinking a sort of transcendental illusion of the gift should not be a simple reproduction of Kant's critical machinery ... neither is it a matter of rejecting that machinery as old fashion'. Even if one wanted to reject it, one is 'in any case ... implicated in it' (Derrida 1994: 30).

Derrida bases his argument about the impossibility of time on Aristotle,[8] but another, perhaps better-known and fuller treatment is that of Saint Augustine. We shall follow the latter here. 'We surely know what we mean when we speak of it [time]', says Saint Augustine. 'We also know what is meant when we hear someone else talking about it.' But although we do know, we do not really know. 'What then is time? Provided that no one asks me, I know. If I want to explain it to an enquirer, I do not know' (1991: 230). We know what time means because we have a preconceptual or intuitive understanding of it but once we begin to think about it we discover that we do not know. We do not know what it means because, as Heidegger says, we lack the concept that will make it meaningful. 'Take the two tenses, past and future', says Saint Augustine:

> How can they 'be' when the past is not now present and the future is not yet present? Yet if the present were always present, it would not pass into the past: it would not be time but eternity. If then, in order to be time at all, the present is so made that it passes into the past, how can we say that this present also 'is'? The cause of its being is that it will cease to be. So indeed we cannot truly say that time exists except in the sense that it tends towards non-existence (1991: 231).

This is a critical passage. Time as the future does not exist because it has not happened yet. Time as the past does not exist either, because it has already happened and is no longer present. And it is clear also that the present cannot always be present because it would be eternity, not time. To be time, time has to come from the future, stay in the present, and then pass into the past. The important question is whether it can linger in the present long enough to be grasped. Saint Augustine considers everyday expressions such as the present century, year, month, day, and so on, but what he finds is that they are not what they say they are. They are not present. A century is not present because some years have already passed and some are still in the future. What is present therefore, what is grasped, is not a *century* but something else. The same logic applies to smaller and smaller units of time until one realises that there is no unit of time, however small, that is not divisible into past and future and hence no unit either that is present as such a unit. Saint Augustine (1991: 232) is forced to conclude, 'If we can think of some bit of time which cannot be divided into even the smallest instantaneous moments, that alone is what we can call "present." And this flies so quickly from future into past that it is an interval with no duration.' Such is the paradox with time. If it has duration, it is divisible into past and future and is therefore not present. If it has no duration it is not present either. Any way one looks at it, time does not appear and cannot be present – which, as we have seen, is not to say that it is nothing.

Much the same can be said about the other present under consideration – the gift. In his critique of Mauss and of 'the anthropologists who quote him or refer to him' – those, that is, who speak of the gift as if it was a real thing and not a phantom – Derrida (1994: 12) turns first to the 'semantic precomprehension' of the word *gift* that common sense and everyday language make available. Everyone understands what gift means and what giving involves, but does anyone know what it is? According to common sense, a gift is something, whether material or symbolic, that someone (an individual or collective subject) gives to someone else. Everyone understands also that for a thing to be gift there must be no reciprocity, exchange, counter-gift, return, or payment of any sort. If something is given in return, there is no gift. This recognition, Derrida points out, is readily available to everyone involved when the cultural protocols are not observed, for example, when the counter-gift is given before the socially prescribed time has elapsed. If a counter-gift is given immediately or soon after the initial gift has been received, it is clear to both gift giver and gift recipient that there is no gift. Without time, says Bourdieu (1977: 6) in his own discussion of the gift, the time that separates gift from counter-gift, there can be no gift. Time 'is what authorises the collectively maintained and approved self-deception without which symbolic exchange, a fake circulation of a fake coin, could not operate'. It could not operate without time because it would be glaringly obvious to the parties involved that the gift is a 'fake'. We should also note here that this 'self-deception' is collectively approved and maintained not only by means of time, that is, the things that the parties involved engage with in the *meantime* and which allows them to forget that the gift is a fake. It is collectively approved and maintained through difference as well. The counter-gift must not only be postponed or, to use the terms that Derrida uses to define *différance*, *deferred*; it must also be different. If it is the same thing as the inaugural gift, it is clear to the parties involved that the gift has not been accepted and is returned to its owner.

How much time does it take for the gift to become a fake? It takes no time at all – for there is no such thing as time. If time itself is nothing, the gift is always already not a gift. Anything more than an instant, 'an instant already caught up in the temporalizing synthesis' says Derrida (1994: 14), anything with duration and therefore divisible into past and future, hence nothing present, is enough to turn the gift into a phantom. Let us take first the case of the gift recipient. If the gift is to be gift, it must not appear to the recipient as gift. If the gift recipient recognises it as gift, at that very instant it is ontologically transformed and is no longer gift. It becomes a *debt* to be repaid. If it does appear as gift then, it is no longer gift. If, on the other hand, it does not appear as a gift, if it is not recognised by the gift recipient as gift, there is no gift either. It must be recognised as a gift to be gift, but as soon as it is recognised, it is no longer gift. Much the same can be said about the gift giver. For a gift to be gift there must be no return, exchange, counter-gift, payment, and so on. The condition of possibility (and impossibility) of the gift is that it must be free and unconditional. But it never is free and this is not only or even mainly because the gift recipient feels obligated to make a counter-gift. Long before the cycle of reciprocity closes in this way, long before the gift recipient has time even to expresses gratitude, the cycle has already closed and the gift is already not a gift. It is always already not a gift. From the moment there is an intention to give, from the moment one becomes aware that what one wishes to do is to give a gift to someone else, at that very moment the gift disappears. There is an automatic return even when the gift giver has no ulterior motives and does not expect a return. What the gift giver takes by giving – prior to and over and above what the gift recipient will give in return – is a symbolic equivalent. It may be the pleasure of knowing that one's gift will make someone else happy, for example, or the recognition that one is doing the right thing. If one recognises that what one is doing or intends to do is giving a gift, the gift is no longer gift. 'At *the limit*', says Derrida (1994: 14), '*the gift as gift* ought *not appear as gift: either to the donner or to the donor*'. If it does appear as gift to either of them, it is instantly transformed into something else. If it does not appear either to the one or the other, it is not (a) present and does not exist. Anyway one looks at it, the gift is nowhere to be seen. It is impossible.

Such is Derrida's argument or at least part of his argument. For, as we have already noted, to say that the gift is impossible is not to deny its existence as a phenomenon. People do give and take what they think of *as* gifts all the time. But whether they know it or not, whether they recognise it or not, what they are dealing with is the phantom of the gift.[9] For they neither give nor take gifts even though they no doubt give and take. 'The gift can certainly keep its phenomenality or, if one prefers, its appearance as gift', Derrida says. 'But its very appearance, the simple phenomenon of the gift annuls it as gift, transforming the apparition into a phantom and the operation into a simulacrum' (1994: 14). If there is no gift the distinction between giving and taking collapses. Giving becomes the same thing as taking, irrespective of whether one wishes it to be taking or not, and taking becomes the same thing as giving, even when what is given in return is only a symbolic equivalent, such as an expression of gratitude. The 'collectively approved and maintained self-deception' notwithstanding, there is no difference between the two and nothing to distinguish gift exchange from any other form of exchange. If so, the gift is another economy, albeit an economy in denial, one still haunted by a phantom. But what exactly is economy?

Etymologically, says Derrida, the term refers to the law of the household and more specifically to the law of distribution and sharing or partition. It no doubt refers also to the market, limitation in spending, saving, and so on. But in addition to or in parallel with these meanings, and more fundamentally, it also names a domain of circulation or circularity in which what goes round comes round. Economy, says Derrida:

> [I]mplies the idea of exchange, of circulation, of return. The figure of the circle is obviously *at the center*, if that can still be said of a circle. It stands at the center of any problematic of *oikonomia*, as it does of any economic field.... This motif of circulation can lead one to think that the law of economy is the – circular – return to the point of departure, to the origin, also to the home (1994: 6–7).

We began with the figure of the circle and we will capitalise on it by extending the problematic of *oikonomia* beyond the economic field and the field of gift exchange in due course. We shall explore in succession the economy of thought, understood both as a limitation in knowing and as the circularity of the known; the political economy, understood as the limitation imposed on autonomy by the circulation of power; and finally, and more broadly, the economy of European thought itself, the thought that, as we have already noted, even though has always already been a circle it was only recently that its going round and coming round in full circle became apparent. For the moment, however, I wish to draw the implications of Derrida's argument with respect to the postcolonial and no doubt colonial and neocolonial claim that European thought is a gift to the rest of the world.

The Power of Giving

If there is no gift there can be no gift of thought either, no gift of European thought or of any other kind of thought for that matter. That is an obvious implication. The gift of European thought emerges as a phantom, and the operation whereby it is given and taken a simulacrum or, to use Bourdieu's terms, a 'collective misrecognition' sustained by reciprocal desire. As we shall see in the following chapters, insofar as European thought claims to have made (a) present to itself what it means to be – among other things and what concerns us here in particular, what it means to be a human being (autonomous) and a society (modern) – it has made nothing present. And insofar as it claims or it is claimed on its behalf to have made present to others as a present these things, it has given them nothing and they have taken nothing. Perhaps 'there is' Being, the Being of the beings we call humanity and society or 'it gives' this Being, but European thought is certainly not the *it* that gives it and, in any case, the it that is being given is itself nothing. It refuses to appear no matter how much anyone tries to make it (a) present. It should not be surprising therefore, that even after the end of colonialism, even more than half a century after the end, the end has not been reached and is nowhere in sight. The gift of European thought is nowhere to be found, and no one can account for it. Europe cannot account for it because it does not have it, which is not to say that it does not pretend to have it and give it generously to the rest of the world. The rest of the world cannot account for it either because it has not been given anything to have, which does not stop it from pretending that it has taken hold of it and made it its own property or, if this leads to far too many glaring contradictions – as it does – it does not stop it from pretending that this gift exists and will materialise one day if only certain bad habits of thought like historicism are broken.

As I have already mentioned, this pretending on both sides of the equation forms the basis of a silent and therefore unrecognised complicity between Europe and its others. And by others I do not mean everyone that Europe considers other. Many if not most people around the world are not concerned with such issues and are not involved in this game of dissimulation. I mean rather those others who consider European thought a gift and cannot stop wanting it, whether they have not given up on it and still hope to possess it one day – in the end and at the end – such as postcolonial critics and other like-minded postcolonial subjectivities, or, less visibly perhaps, *have* given up hope and emphatically reject it in a gesture that repeats the sour-grapes-syndrome. To paraphrase Bourdieu (1984), because Europe and these others agree on the stakes involved, it makes no difference whether one chooses to emphasise the disagreements that divide them in complicity or the complicity that unites them in disagreement. At the end of the day what matters is the agreement, because without it there would be no grounds for engagement and disagreement. This complicity between Europe and its others needs to be underscored and recognised for at least two reasons. It needs to be recognised firstly, because it exposes the pretentions of postcolonial discourse as a critique of European thought as well as the secret desire harboured by those who apparently reject it, often vehemently and violently. Secondly, and more importantly, it needs to be recognised because it accounts, at least partly, for what has become possible again after decades of silence, utterable and reproducible, namely, not only to defend empire publicly but also to take up the cause for a new kind of imperialism that would bring to the rest of the world, among other gifts, stability and liberty. In a world in which no one doubts that European thought is a gift, least of all postcolonial critics, it was perhaps a matter of time for such discourses to appear and circulate as a serious and legitimate statement.

This new imperialism has been dubbed postmodern and refers to the relationship that the postmodern world, meaning Europe and more broadly the West, ought to establish with the rest of the world, which apparently is less than postmodern – for otherwise there would be no need for a new imperialism. Part of the rest of the world, we are told, is modern and part, the rest of the rest, pre-modern (Cooper n.d.). It is clear, to anthropologists at least, that the new imperialism is premised on the assumption that the world can be divided on the basis of three evolutionary stages, and in this respect there is nothing new about it. Imperialist discourses of the nineteenth century operated with exactly the same assumption, even if the terminology was different: civilisation, barbarism, and savagery, respectively. Be that as it may, as these are postmodern times, at least in the postmodern world, the new imperialism cannot be a simple reincarnation of the old. For one thing, as its proponents argue, it is consistent with human rights and cosmopolitan values. For another, it is not interested in colonising other lands. What it wishes to do, it seems, is only to give, not to take or, at any rate, not to take without making certain that it also gives. It is worth quoting here at some length:

> What form should intervention take? The most logical way to deal with chaos, and the one most often employed in the past, is colonisation. But colonisation is unacceptable to *postmodern states* (and, as it happens, to some *modern states* too). It is precisely because of the death of imperialism that we see the emergence of the *pre-modern world*. Empire and imperialism are terms of abuse in the postmodern world. ... All the conditions for imperialism are there, but both the supply and demand for it have dried up. And yet the weak still need the strong and the strong still need an orderly world. A world in which the efficient and the well-governed export *stability and liberty* [giving], and which is open to investment and growth [taking]. ... What is needed is a new kind of imperialism acceptable to a world of human rights and cosmopolitan values (Cooper 2002: 17; my emphases).

This is not a lonely voice. There are other discourses that express similar sentiments, and here I will explore briefly one that is perhaps more nuanced, a discourse that acknowledges the dark side of the old of imperialism, the 'Bad Things' (Ferguson 2004: xvii) that happened during colonial times: the *taking* of slaves, lives, land, resources, and so on. Yet this should not be taken as another example of magnanimity on the part of the 'postmodern world'. The latter has nothing to lose and much to gain from such an acknowledgement. It gives the rest of the world – an implicit apology for the bad things associated with colonialism – and because it gives, it also takes. What it gains is the profits of recognition for its democratic openness and open-mindedness, its commitment to human rights and cosmopolitan values. By acknowledging the transgression of these rights and values, it confirms itself first and foremost in its own eyes that it is, indeed, what it claims to be – open-minded, democratic, and postmodern. In any case, acknowledgement of the bad things is not the ultimate aim of such discourses. What they give with one hand, they take with the other. They want the 'good things' about colonialism acknowledged as well.

The new imperialism or neoimperialism operates with the common-sense assumption that giving is one thing and taking another. And because it does, it thinks that it can create a balance sheet for empire in which the credit side outweighs the debit side. Having acknowledged the taking, it turns to the giving – among other things, law and order, free markets, representative institutions, and above all 'the idea of liberty' (Ferguson 2004: xxiii) – and argues that when everything is counted and accounted for, what the colonisers gave to the rest of the world exceeds by far what they took from it. This excess – 'the accursed share', as Betaille (1988) might say – is the gift of the colonisers to the colonised. Hence, the conclusion: empire was a 'Good Thing' (Ferguson 2004: xxi). And hence the lesson to be learned: in a suitably adjusted form, a form that takes into account postmodern sensitivities, it is precisely what the contemporary world urgently needs – a postmodern empire.

This sort of accounting is not unique to the new imperialism. The old imperialists took stock as well, even if they could find nothing to enter on the debit side of the balance sheet. For the apologists of empire, colonialism gave without taking anything in return, except perhaps the 'old reward', as Kipling says in his famous poem, 'The White Man's Burden', namely, 'the blame of those ye better, the hate of those ye guard'.[10] Finally, the same sort of accounting logic has been used in the critique of colonialism and imperialism but in reverse: the colonisers took without giving anything in return, or if they did give something it was far less than what they took. This is the view of the Marxist version of the critique, which understands colonialism first and foremost as economic exploitation. But it is not uncommon in the postcolonial version that understands it, in addition, as a form of symbolic exploitation. A paradigmatic example is Edward Said's famous argument that 'European culture *gained* in strength and identity by setting itself off against the Orient as a sort of surrogate and even underground self' (1979: 3; my emphasis). On the basis of the common-sense logic used here, European culture could only have gained in its encounter with the Orient either by taking from it without giving anything back or by taking more than what it gave.

This familiar picture is radically transformed when one begins to treat giving and taking not as opposite but equivalent and interchangeable notions. To begin with the last example, if giving is also taking and taking also giving, European culture could not have taken from the Orient without giving anything in return. If it took from it something, it also gave it something. But what about the gain? On the basis of the accounting logic we have been discussing, this could have only been the outcome of having taken from the Orient more than it had given it. We will deal with this point shortly. For the moment, we may wonder what European culture might have given the Orient by means of taking from it. The issue here is identity and, as is often said – which is not to say that the implications of what is being said are always fully grasped – identities are relational. They are relational because it is impossible to identify oneself directly, to constitute oneself as a subject that knows what it is by means of one's own devices – an auto-identification, which, and let us underscore this point, is based on the same logic that considers auto-gifts of thought (truth and autonomy) possible. We have being saying that there are no such devices and it would seem that when it comes to the question of auto-identification at least, many would agree that every identification occurs by way of another. Our contention is that this is precisely the case also with the question of truth and autonomy.

If there can be no auto-identification, it should be clear that without the Orient (or some such) playing the role of the other, Europe would not have been able to constitute its identity as it did and become what it thinks it is, let alone gain in strength as a result of the encounter. If it gained strength, it also lost strength, at least insofar as it became dependent on the Orient as a surrogate, underground self. This much has now been recognised, and we shall mention here in this respect Bhabha's (1984) critique of Said's early work, particularly the critique of the idea that colonial discourse is sovereign. No doubt, it is capable of constituting the Orient or some such as Europe's underground self. Yet the foundation of this edifice is inherently unstable. Without the other recognising itself as other and European thought as a gift, it would collapse.

Let us now turn to the question of whether Europe gained in strength and identity by taking from the Orient more than what it gave in return. We have already noted that there is no taking that is not also a giving, that does not create some sort of debt or dependence. It follows from this that the more one takes the more one gives. By the same token, if one takes more than what one gives in return, one gives more than what one takes – gives in and up as we have said. To see why this is so, we need only turn to Marcel Mauss's famous essay, *The Gift*, and introduce two quotations. The first one reads as follows: 'The obligation of worthy return is *imperative*. Face is *lost for ever* if it is not made or if equivalent value is not destroyed' (Mauss 1967: 41; my emphases). In the second quotation Mauss (1967: 72) notes the following: 'To accept without returning or repaying more is to face subordination, to become a client and subservient, to become *minister*.' In the first quotation a 'worthy return' is defined as giving back as much as one takes, something of equivalent value or, as in the case of the potlatch to which this quotation refers, destroying things of equivalent value. If this imperative is not observed, if one does not give anything back or gives less than what one takes, which is to say, if one takes more than what one gives, one gives more than what one takes. One loses face, says Mauss, and loses it 'for ever' – which constitutes a form of social death, as we have noted in the first chapter. The loss of one's dignity and respect, self-respect perhaps, certainly the respect of others is the price to pay for taking without giving or for not giving as much. It is what one gives up, and what transforms taking more than what one gives in return into giving more than what one takes to begin with. The same considerations apply to the second case. It should be obvious from the quotation itself that the price to pay in this instance is one's autonomy. By taking more than what one gives back, one gives more than what one takes. One becomes minister – a minor and a servant – which is to say, one gives in to the giver and gives up whatever independence one may have had. If that is the case, Europe could not have gained in strength in its encounter with the Orient by taking more than what it gave. If it did gain, it is because it gave more than it took or, at any rate, convinced itself and, more fundamentally, the Orient that it did, namely, civilisation.

This brings me to the neoimperialist claim we have already encountered, namely, that the colonisers gave to the rest of the world more than what they took from it and that, therefore, according to its accounting logic, empire was a good thing. It brings me also to a certain paradox associated with the so-called white man's burden, the fact that although this 'man' received nothing in return for the gifts he gave to the colonised except blame and hatred, he nonetheless insisted on and persisted in giving generously to them. How is this to be explained? We shall examine each in turn, but let us note here in a preliminary fashion that if giving is also taking (and taking also giving), as we have been saying, to give more than what one takes is to take more than what one gives, much the same way that to take more than what one gives is to give more than what ones takes. Let us recall, to begin with, that as Mauss says 'to give is to show one's superiority, to show that one is something more and higher, that one is *magister*' (1967: 72). Let us recall also Derrida's point in an otherwise tortured sentence: that through the 'gesture of the gift' the subject seeks 'to constitute its own unity and, precisely, to get its own identity recognised so that that identity comes back to it, so that it can reappropriate its identity: as its own property' (1994: 11) – which is a reappropriation, he says later, 'with surplus-value, a certain capitalization' (1994: 101). All this suggests that giving is taking not simply or even mainly because there may be a counter-gift but also and more fundamentally, because through it one confirms oneself, both in one's own eyes and those of others, in one's superior position and identity. It is, in short, a double take. That giving turns out to be more profitable than taking has been known in imperialist circles for a long time, which is not to say known necessarily explicitly and consciously. And it renders the idea of a white man's burden not so much a lie that hides the truth of exploitation as the argument from ideology would have it, as a truth that hides the lie or 'collective misrecognition' of the gift as gift. Of all the examples that one could marshal as evidence of an awareness of the profitability of giving among imperialist circles, I have chosen a passage from Ferguson that quotes Winston Churchill musing, 'as a young man, fresh from his first colonial war', about the empire:

> What enterprise that an *enlightened* community may attempt is more *noble* and more *profitable* than the reclamation from *barbarism* of fertile regions and large populations? To *give* peace to warring tribes, to administer justice where all was violence, to strike the chains off the slave, to draw the richness from the soil, to plant the earliest seeds of commerce and learning, to increase in whole peoples their capacities for pleasure and diminish their chances for pain – what more *beautiful ideal* or more valuable *reward* can inspire human effort? (2004: xxvii; my emphases).

For Churchill then, to give – peace, justice, liberty, prosperity, education, in a word, civilisation – to those who were in need was the most noble thing that an enlightened community could ever do, the most beautiful ideal to inspire human effort. Yet it should be clear from the passage that this giving is hardly a disinterested act. Through giving, one also takes – and takes at the same time. Although the most noble, this enterprise is also the most profitable; although the most beautiful and pure ideal, what inspires human effort in addition is the fact that giving promises the most valuable reward. The reward, it should be clear, is precisely the confirmation of the enlightened community as such a community – enlightened, civilised, and hence superior to the purported barbarian populations to which it gives. This realisation – that the noble is also profitable, the disinterested ideal also a means to a valuable reward, in short, that giving is taking with a certain capitalisation – took time to register. In its early days the empire prioritised taking, appropriating what did not belong to it through force and violence. But the realisation did finally register, and the process was eventually reversed. Here is how Ferguson describes this change:

> In the eighteenth century the British Empire had been, at best, *amoral*. The Hanoverians had grabbed power in Asia, land in America and slaves in Africa. Native peoples were either taxed, robbed or wiped out.... The Victorians had more *elevated aspirations*. They *dreamt* not just of ruling the world, but of redeeming it. It was *no longer enough* for them to exploit other races; now the aim became to improve them. Native peoples themselves would cease to be exploited, but their cultures – superstitious, backward, heathen – would have to go. In particular, the Victorians *aspired* to bring light to what they called the Dark Continent (Ferguson 2003: 113; my emphases).

Exploiting other races may have been profitable, but by the nineteenth century it became apparent that it was no longer enough. To capitalise fully on the empire the Victorians had to find other means of securing profit. Paradoxical as it may sound, they reversed the strategy of the previous generation, and rather than taking from the native populations, they began giving to them instead. What they gave them was 'light'. And they gave it to them because in addition to ruling the world they also wanted to redeem it. That was now their dream and elevated aspiration. Compared to the Hanoverians, Fergusson suggests, the Victorians became moral. He assumes that morality was the catalyst for this change because he thinks of giving as the opposite of taking, as a practice inspired by the 'purer sentiments', as Mauss (1967: 66) says – 'charity, social service and solidarity' – or, as Churchill says, by nobility of spirit and beautiful ideals. But there is nothing moral, pure, or noble about it. Taking may be good too, at least in the short run, but in the long run it turns into a liability. The Victorians seem to have understood this at some level. They seem to have realised that in the long run nothing is more profitable than giving.

Let us return to the neoimperialist attempt to set the record straight about the empire. The Hanoverians took but the Victorians gave, and they gave more than what the Hanoverians took. Hence, overall the empire was a good thing, and because it was good it ought to be revived, no doubt in a suitably adjusted form, in line with the sensitivities of the postmodern world. It should be clearer now why the argument falls flat. If giving is the same as taking, as everyone we have been talking about seems to agree, each in its own way, no doubt – Malinowski, Derrida, Mauss, Churchill, not to mention Locke and Kant to whom we will turn in the next chapter – if giving is the same as taking then, giving more than what one takes is taking more than what one gives; or, to put it in another way, taking less than what one gives is giving less than what one takes. Whichever way one chooses to look at it, the point is that the empire became truly profitable by giving, not taking. This structure goes some way in explaining the paradox with the white man's burden. As Kipling's poem says, the white man shouldered this burden – sent his 'sons to exile', asked them to 'wait in heavy harness' and to 'seek another's profit' and so on – knowing too well that the only reward he will ever receive is 'the blame of those ye better, the hate of those ye guard'. Is the white man a saint or a fool? He is neither, of course. In giving everything without taking anything in return, he took everything by giving nothing. In making the ultimate sacrifice, seemingly choosing the other over himself, the white man reaped the ultimate reward. He vested himself with the power of giving.

As we have seen, at the beginning of his discussion on the impossibility of the gift Derrida refers to the king's morganatic wife and her desire to give the rest of her time to Saint-Cyr, the charitable institution. But she cannot do so because the rest of her time refers to time itself, which does not appear and is nothing and which therefore she does not have and will never be able to have. Nonetheless, says Derrida, this is what she would like to do. She desires time itself 'not for herself but so as to be able to give it'. We may wonder why. Perhaps, says Derrida, 'for the power of giving ... so as to give herself this power of giving' (1994: 4). How then, is this power to be understood? What does it mean to give time, not one's time, which as we said refers to what one does in the meantime, but time itself? If time as such is the condition of possibility of everything that happens in the meantime, the space that the absence of time opens up for anything to happen, then giving time itself can only mean giving everything, which is also nothing. It can only mean making present as a present to the world Being itself – which is nothing but *there is*. This is pure creation, creation in the biblical sense. And it is power itself. It is the ability to create something out of nothing – by speaking it – without having to take anything beforehand – because by definition there is no before – and hence also the ability to give it without taking anything in return.

Perhaps this is also the imperial desire: to give everything and to take nothing, which is to say, to give nothing and to take everything.

Notes

1. 'I did not want to write the standard modernization story of progress from constraint to freedom.... As I wrote, however, I found that I could not avoid using the words "traditional" and "modern", however hard I tried.... Even as tried to use substitute terms, such as "then" and "now", "village" and "urban", or "agrarian" and "bourgeois", I found myself reproducing the problematic traditional/modernity contrast, reinforcing the vision of tradition as modernity's devalued opposite' (Collier 1997: 10).

2. For an interesting twist in the story of the gift as poison, see Parry (1989).

3. This point is by now well established. See among others Chatterjee's (1986) excellent study of Indian nationalism as a derivative discourse.

4. The term *postcolonial revenge* is quoted approvingly from the work of another postcolonial critic. 'Nowhere is this book motivated by a desire for postcolonial revenge. It does not seek finally to marginalise the West' (Gandhi 1998: x).

5. As Young (2001) rightly observes, we speak of postcolonialism but not of postimperialism.

6. See for relevant discussion in particular Lukes's (1969: 23) translation of Durkheim's 'Individualism and the Intellectuals'. I raised the question of this religion and what has come to replace it more recently by incorporating it in a grander scheme of things in Argyrou (2005).

7. See discussion in the 'Preface to the Second Edition' of *Critique of Pure Reason* (Kant 1999 [1781]: 106–124).

8. For a detailed discussion see '*Ousia* and *Gramme*: Note on a Note from *Being and Time*' (1982: 29–67).

9. 'If the system [of symbolic exchange] is to work', says Bourdieu (1977: 6), 'the agents must not be entirely unaware of the truth of their exchanges ... while at the same time they must refuse to know and above all recognize it'.

10. Quoted in Ferguson (2004: 380a).

CHAPTER 3

THE ECONOMY OF THOUGHT

The Phenomenon and the Phantom

Although perceptions have changed somewhat over the years, it is still the case that Derrida's critique of the 'metaphysics of presence', of the possibility of time as the present and hence the possibility also of the gift and of the gift of thought as a present, is understood in certain academic circles as an example of postmodern irrationalism that threatens to destroy the foundations of knowledge and truth. These are the 'Knights of the Good and the True', says Caputo (1997: 38) in his defence of Derrida, the pillars of rationality. It is not uncommon, he says, with perhaps a touch of the dramatic in his portrayal of this critique:

> to portray Derrida as the devil himself, a street-corner anarchist, a relativist, or subjectivist, or nihilist, out to destroy our traditions and institutions, our beliefs and values, to mock philosophy and truth itself, to undo everything the Enlightenment has done—and to replace all this with wild nonsense and irresponsible play (Caputo 1997: 36).

For Caputo (1997: 37) the assumption that deconstruction leads to 'a kind of anarchistic relativism in which "anything goes"' is a serious misunderstanding of what Derrida has been trying to achieve. Not everything goes and not everything is relative. There is a set of unconstructed and hence 'undeconstructible' intuitions or preconceptions – among them, 'justice, the gift, hospitality, the *tout autre, l'àvenir*' (Caputo 1997: 128) – that guide deconstruction as a critical project and arrest the possible effects of 'anarchistic relativism'. Hence, says Caputo (1997: 42), although 'highly unconventional' and the bad press it has received notwithstanding, deconstruction is in effect an antiessentialist critique. Its business is not to destroy 'our' traditions and institutions but to 'open and loosen things up'.

Put in this way, Derrida's critical project appears almost harmless, but it is not at all clear whether such an argument could allay fears of epistemological and ethical relativism. Note, for instance, how Caputo himself refers to the 'undeconstructible' (as he ought to do if he is to be true to Derrida's argument): 'the undeconstructible', he says, 'if such a thing exists...' (1997: 42). This is precisely the question – does such a thing exist? As we have seen in the previous chapter, preconceptions or intuitions are beyond everyone's grasp. Perhaps 'there is' justice, the gift, hospitality, and so on, but none of these 'things' exist. Perhaps 'it gives' all these 'things' and more but both the 'it' that does the giving and the given are nothing. They are not present and can never become (a) present in society and history, and to think otherwise would be to slip into the 'metaphysics of presence' which Derrida has been at pains to debunk. Derrida's own metaphysics is the exact opposite – a 'metaphysics of absence'. It is the metaphysics of radical human finitude where, as we have seen, fundamental preconceptions such as Being, time, and the gift are given to thought to think but only as the impossible, only as that which can never be grasped, in the double sense of this sense – neither understood nor taken hold of. It is the status of these so-called undeconstructibles as a permanent absence that raises doubts about their presumed ability to arrest the effects of epistemological and ethical relativism. If no one can grasp the Being of beings, including the being that Derrida calls justice, how can anyone ever use it to defend knowledge of particular beings, to speak of the truth and make moral judgments?

Derrida's own denials of the charge of relativism do not inspire much confidence either:

> This way of thinking context does not, as such, amount to relativism, with everything that is sometimes associated with it (skepticism, empiricism, even nihilism). First of all because ... relativism, like all its derivatives, remains a philosophical position in contradiction with itself. Second, because this 'deconstructive way' of thinking context is neither a philosophical position nor a critique of finite contexts, which it analyses without claiming any absolute view (Derrida 1988: 137).

Derrida is right, of course, in saying that relativism is a self-contradictory philosophical position. The question, however, is not whether one holds and advocates this position but whether relativism has one in its own grasp. As to the second point, it may indeed be the case that one's analyses imply an absolute view, but how can one claim to hold such a view when one also claims that there are only contexts? – 'the phrase which for some has become a sort of slogan ... of deconstruction ("there is nothing outside the text"), means nothing else: there is nothing outside context' (Derrida 1988: 136). The problem of relativism then cannot be brushed aside so easily, and if there is something for which 'the Nights of the Good and the True' should be criticised, this is not their concern with his problem. They should be concerned. It is, rather, their short-sightedness, the selective memory they employ in holding Derrida and other postmodernists responsible for opening Pandora's box. The box was opened long before them. The 'metaphysics of absence', hence, also subjectivism and relativism, has been the most fundamental premise of European thought from the beginning – if the beginning is what is called the Enlightenment. It was the beginning of European thought as we understand it today, and it is also its end – both its *telos* and its limit – the condition of possibility of any critique. As we shall see in more detail shortly, it was a beginning that by all accounts began with Locke's denial of innate ideas and the possibility of grasping real essences and culminated in the Kantian denial of the possibility of grasping things in themselves.

This, let us hasten to add, is not to say that Derrida is Lockeian or Kantian, whatever such a claim could possibly mean. But in not saying this, we should not be blinded either to the profound continuities between them, so many in fact that Caputo is sometimes tempted to underplay the differences somewhat. 'Part of the difference between the old and the new Enlightenment [Locke, Kant (and others), on the one hand, and Derrida, on the other] is a question of style. Derrida's more *avant-garde* style makes the old *Aufklärers* [which I take to mean the contemporary proponents of the old lights] nervous, even when their aims are often the same as his' (1997: 54). That may well be the case, but as Caputo also knows, there is a more profound and fundamental difference. Derrida has been more true to the Enlightenment than the old lights, if not to its letter, certainly to its spirit – the spirit of critique. He sought to take critique to its logical conclusion – and did so persistently and consistently. The spectre of relativism, then, has been haunting European thought from the beginning, and to see this one need only consider the eighteenth-century reactions to Locke's epistemology – which we will do below – not to say anything about the reactions to Hume. Allowing for the differences in language and the concern with religion, the latter could be easily mistaken for the contemporary reactions to Derrida, at least as Caputo depicts them.[1]

Let us return to the possibility of grasping, of understanding and possessing, hence, the possibility of giving and taking also, because this will be the point of entry into the discussion that follows on what we shall call 'the economy of thought', the possibility of the gift and what concerns us here in particular, the possibility of the gift of thought. My contention in this chapter is that European thought has been constituted in such a way that for it there can be no gift of thought – if, that is, by gift we understand what one subject (individual or collective) gives to another. For, apparently, people often talk also about gifts that they make to themselves. European thought does this too; and it does it catachrestically, by contradicting itself. Although it makes it a point to demonstrate the impossibility of the gift of thought, at the same time it takes it for granted (as a grant or gift, no doubt) that the subject is capable of giving to itself and that it ought to do so at all times. As we shall below, this presumed giving, which can only be described as an act of auto-generosity and autonomy, is what Kant defined as enlightenment. On the one hand, then, there is no gift of thought for European thought; on the other, the subject can give to itself and take from itself – an auto-gift of thought, as we have said – as if the subject can exist independently, cut off from everything else and everyone else, as if it can generate everything it needs to think with from nothing, as if, in short, it can step outside history and time.

To be fair, European thought has never broached the question of the gift of thought directly – and certainly never used the term *gift* to describe transmission of knowledge, passing on information, giving advice, and so on. What it has done was to make what we are calling here the economy of thought an issue – and a fundamental one at that, the very backdrop from which it emerged as an intellectual tradition. Yet economy is the reverse of the gift, and wherever there is economy, which is everywhere – and let this not be misunderstood as an economistic or neoliberalist claim – the gift is impossible. To arrive at the impossibility of the gift of thought, therefore, we must read European thought backward, from what it has to say about the economy of thought to what, what it says suggests about the gift of thought. Let us then begin by pointing out that the economy of thought is an economy not because knowledge is bought and sold, although apparently it can be an economy for this reason too. Rather, I use the term to refer, in the first instance, to the limitations imposed on what can be grasped in the face of the desire to grasp everything and, as we have seen in the case of the king's morganatic wife, the desire also to give everything. This, no doubt, is also the scholastic desire. The scholar wishes to grasp everything and to give everything, which is not to say grasp everything there is necessarily, but everything there is to grasp about a particular object of study, namely, its truth. A parallel to the economy of thought in the sense of limitation – for there is another sense to which I will turn below – is the economy of positive economics. In this case, too, unlimited desire comes up against limited resources. There is so much that can be produced with what is available and hence so many human wants that can be satisfied. For every national economy or for economy in general there is at any given point in time a 'production-possibility boundary', a line that marks the limits of productive capacity and charts the different combinations of choice – more of one thing necessarily means less of another.

The positive thinking that underpins positive economics is the kind of thinking that underpins the economy of thought as well. This is the thinking that criticised pure thought as speculative fancy, took stock of the resources available, and drew a clear 'knowledge production-possibility boundary'. On the inside of this boundary lies everything that thought can possibly grasp, everything empirical and historical. On the outside lies what is beyond experience, everything metaphysical and transcendental – real essences, things in themselves, Being and time would be some of the terms that philosophers used to designate the ungraspable. This boundary is no doubt flexible. It can expand outward as more things become known, the same way that it expands in the market economy as a result of an increase in productive capacity. What can never happen, however, is the elimination of the boundary itself as boundary. Desire will never be eradicated no matter how many wants the economy satisfies; what lies on the other side of the knowledge production-possibility boundary will never be grasped no matter how much knowledge of the empirical increases. If we were to put a date to the first sketching of this knowledge production-possibility boundary, the first clear-cut separation of the empirical from the transcendental, this would be by all accounts the late seventeenth century. And if we were to put a name to the sketch, it would be the name of John Locke. From Locke's time onwards, the dominant paradigm in the European intellectual tradition will maintain that thought can do no more than grasp phenomena. It may still desire to grasp the essence of things, things in themselves, Being and time, but it can neither understand nor take hold of them. From Locke's time onwards such 'things' cannot be present in the empirical world, and the desire to make them (a) present is destined to remain unfulfilled.

This brings me to the second sense in which I will be using the term economy of thought. It is the sense that Derrida uses in his analysis of the gift – economy as circulation or exchange, a domain in which giving is taking and taking giving, the circle where what is given always already comes back to the giver in one form or another and what is taken is always already marked by the intention of return. As I will try to show in the next section, economy in this sense has also been a fundamental premise of European thought from the beginning, notably in Locke's epistemology and Kant's political writings. Not that Locke or Kant necessarily conceptualised the giving and taking of what reason can grasp as a circle. What they said about it seems to have been based on experience and common sense, and there has been no attempt to theorise the issue. Had they done so, as Derrida clearly did, they would have realised perhaps that if there is no gift of thought – because there is no pure reason to grasp it – there is no gift of thought across the board, that it is just as impossible to give this gift to another subject as to give it to oneself. Be that as it may, and although they did not say it in so many words, both Locke and Kant insisted that when it comes to thought, giving is a form of taking and taking a form of giving – a giving in and a giving up, as we have said. I shall return to the economy of thought understood as a circle in the next section. For now the discussion will focus on the economy of thought as a limitation to what thought can actually grasp.

The story of how this particular manifestation of the economy of thought emerged is quite well known, even if it is not known by the terms that I am using here. A few friends, we read, met in the chamber of one of the members of the group to discuss morality and revealed religion. Although there are grounds to dispute the accuracy of the date of this meeting, it is said to have taken place in the winter of 1673.[2] Having made no headway at all in their discussion, having gone round and round in circles—we might say—it occurred to one of the friends that they may have taken the wrong course, that perhaps the circle with which they had encircled themselves could be avoided. It occurred to him that before launching into a discussion of complex issues of this nature it was more prudent to examine whether there were any prospects of success, whether human thought was equipped to provide answers to such questions, whether morality and God were things that could be known. It was a matter of thinking economically, no doubt, positively and rationally, of aligning means to ends, of taking stock of the resources available and making a decision as to how they could be more productively employed – a question, in short, of establishing an economy of thought. This change of course he proposed to his friends and 'all readily assented', says Locke (1997 [1706]: 8), 'whereupon it was agreed, that this should be our first enquiry'. Locke wrote down some 'hasty and undigested thoughts' for the next meeting, and this, he tells us, was the beginning of *An Essay Concerning Human Understanding*. For all we know then, the *Essay* was the outcome of an ordinary encounter among philosophically minded friends. Yet ordinary as its beginnings may have been, it launched European thought as we know it.

Let us follow in broad outline the moves that Locke makes in sketching out the economy of thought (as limitation to what can be known). In the first book of the *Essay* he sets out to demonstrate that there is no such thing as pure thought, no thought that has not always already come into contact with the empirical, hence, contaminated by it – indeed, no thought that has not been the product of the empirical, however indirectly. The argument is what has come to be known as the doctrine of the blank slate, the notion that, as Locke himself put it, the human mind is 'white paper, void of all characters, without any ideas' (1997: 109). There is no pure thought precisely because there are no pure or innate ideas to think with, no characters imprinted on the mind by the hand of God that could be used with the absolute certainty provided by the origin and foundation. There are no original and foundational ideas, no gift of nature in this sense, only the ability of the mind to create its own ideas, to fill the white paper with the characters that it itself invents. Not even the idea of God is innate, Locke will argue, and if this particular idea is not innate, no other idea can possibly be. It stands to reason: 'If God had set any impression, any character on the understanding of men, it is most reasonable to expect it should have been some clear and uniform idea of Himself, as far as our weak capacities were capable to receive so incomprehensible and infinite an object' (1997: 100). Yet there is not such idea, not only because in many nations – 'in Brasil, in Boranday, and the Caribee Islands' (1997: 94) – knowledge of God is absent but also because where it exists it is neither clear nor uniform, and people cannot agree on how it should be understood. Let us note here that Locke does not deny the existence of God, even though he was accused of atheism.[3] His argument, rather, is that the mind discovers God by itself, through its own devices. To the extent that God is known, to the extent that anything at all is known, it is not by way of a timeless gift of nature in the form of innate ideas and principles but through the empirical, which is to say, by means of the ideas that the mind produces in time and in the meantime.

The aim of the first book of the *Essay*, then, is to temporalize thought, which is to say, denaturalise and historicise it. It is to cut it off from the timeless and the transcendental and let it loose in the world of the here and now to labour and produce its own ideas by the sweat of its brow – an epistemological fall from grace, no doubt. This is apparently a radical severing and a costly move because the ideas that the mind produces by itself can never attain the certainty of the ideas imprinted on the mind by God. If it is the mind that constructs them, it can also deconstruct them; if these ideas are not a *given* (gift of nature), there is no reason why they should be *taken* (for granted, as a grant or gift). We shall have to wait until the next section to explore the rationale of this move. Let us note here briefly that this radical severing can be read in more than one way, not only as a fall from grace but also as a weaning off, a matter of coming of age or maturing, as Kant was to say a century later. Having shown that the mind is much poorer than what was usually assumed, having argued that the resources presumed to be available to it are nothing – nothing present on the white paper – Locke turns to consider where ideas come from and what the mind can hope to know with any degree of certainty. We shall not concern ourselves here with the detailed argumentation of the *Essay*. For the purposes of the present discussion, it should suffice to note two things. First, for Locke ideas are the product of the encounter of the mind with the empirical world, what happens during the life of the mind, which is to say, as we have already said, what happens in time or in the meantime. All ideas are the product of experience, however complex and far removed from the empirical world they may seem. They emerge, Locke says, when the mind takes 'notice' of external objects to begin with and in time as the mind develops, when it takes notice also of its own internal operations. '*External objects furnish the mind with ideas of sensible qualities*, which are all those different perceptions they produce in us: and the *mind furnishes the understanding with ideas of its own operations*' (1997: 110). The former is a matter of sensation, the latter a matter of reflection.

The second thing we should note concerns Locke's discussion of the distinction between 'accidents' and 'substances', the sensible qualities of objects perceived by the mind and the question of whether they exist by themselves or are the manifestation of some deeper and hidden reality. 'We accustom ourselves', says Locke, 'to suppose some *substratum*, wherein they do subsist, and from which they do result; which therefore we call substance' (1997: 268). Although Locke considers the idea of substance of little use in philosophy, he is nonetheless unable to do without this custom. And with good reason. As Kant was to put the matter in his own discussion of these issues, 'if we cannot cognize … objects as things in themselves, we at least must be able to *think* them as things in themselves'. We must be able to imagine them because otherwise we would have to accept 'the absurd proposition that there is an appearance without something that appears' (1999[1787]: 115) – the proposition, in other words, that things appear out of nothing. What Locke argues against, then, is not the supposition that substances support accidents – or 'the ontological reality' of substances, as Yolton says in *Locke and the Way of Ideas* – but the epistemological claim that they can be known. Locke himself pleads ignorance – 'I know not' – and does so in the manner of someone who is certain that he cannot be proven wrong – by flaunting his ignorance: '[N]or shall [I] be ashamed to my own ignorance, till they that ask, show me a clear distinct idea of *substance*' (1997: 168). No one has such an idea. The European philosopher may pretend to have it, but he is in no better position than anyone else. He is no better than the Indian philosopher, for example, who claimed that the Earth was supported by an elephant and was asked, presumably to be teased, what supported the elephant only to reply that it rested on broad-backed tortoise. And when he was pressed even further to say where the tortoise itself rested, he 'replied, [on] something, he knew not what'. Nor is the European philosopher any better than children who:

> being questioned, what such a things is, which they know not, readily give this satisfactory answer, that it is *something*; which in truth signifies no more, when so used, either by children or men, but that they know not what; and that the thing they pretend to know, and talk of, is what they have no distinct idea of at all, and so are perfectly ignorant of it, and in the dark (1997: 268).

Although Locke supposes that the substance or the essence of things is something, he also argues that it is nothing – nothing that anyone knows or can know. If it is given to thought to think about, as Derrida says about the gift, if thought must suppose it in order to avoid absurd propositions, as Kant argues, it can think about it only as an impossible being – a permanent absence.

In the related discussion of 'nominal' and 'real' essences, the perceived nature of objects as opposed to their real constitution that remains hidden, Locke comes close to suggesting reasons for this incurable ignorance. His discussion anticipates in some ways the argument that Vico was to develop a few decades later, namely, that we can know with certainty only what we ourselves have made. For Vico this is 'the world of civil society' as opposed to 'the world of nature, which, since God made it, He alone knows' (1984 [1744]: 96). Locke's discussion concerns 'man' and the question of his real constitution. It is possible, he says, that angels have knowledge of 'man's' real essence 'and 'tis certain his Maker has [such knowledge]'. But 'man' himself cannot know what he truly is. He cannot because he is not his own maker. His situation, Locke suggests, is no different from that of the countryman gazing at the 'famous clock of Strasbourg'. The clock's maker 'knows all the springs, wheels, and other contrivances within' but the countryman who comes to town and looks at it 'barely sees the motion of the hand, and hears the clock strike, and observes only some of the outward appearances' (1997: 393–394). The ignorance of the countryman about the clock's internal constitution is equivalent to 'man's' ignorance of his own essence and of the nature of world in general, a manifestation of the finitude of the human condition. 'Man' has not made the world, and he himself has been made. The best he can do therefore is to take notice of, and get to know outward appearances. The internal constitution of things will always eludes him, despite his best efforts.

This, then, is in broad outline the economy of thought that Locke established in the *Essay*, the knowledge production-possibility boundary he drew with a steady hand in the last decades of the seventeenth century. It was no doubt a fateful gesture, an irreversible process, a momentous event destined to guide European thought ever since – an event that marked it irrevocably and to the core. For whatever the subsequent developments in the history of European thought, whatever the occasional reversals and counterarguments, the limitations imposed on the mind in the late seventeenth century as to what it can grasp and therefore give were never to be lifted, the division between the empirical and the transcendental was to become even more firmly entrenched. To see this, to appreciate how far Locke's overall argument is taken for granted today, one need only consider the kind of worldview the *Essay* was arguing against. It would not fail to strike the contemporary reader as alien and naïve. Yolton's study of the intellectual and cultural milieu of Locke's time provides numerous examples, but here I shall refer to only one. It concerns the reactions against Locke's fundamental distinction between nominal and real essences. Locke's critics, says Yolton, 'had no doubts concerning our knowledge of the real essence of things'. Their confidence was based on religious truths, and the case of one Oliver Hill, who put forward the following argument, is characteristic of the prevalent mode of reasoning: 'That Mankind hath some knowledge of the true Essence of things, and adequate ideas, appears to me very plain from *Adam* in *Paradise*, giving names to all the Beasts according to their Nature.' As for those who sought to take most of the sting out of Locke's argument by 'reducing it to a common-sense recognition of the limitations of human knowledge', Yolton has this to say: 'Locke was not merely saying that we know some things about natural objects and are ignorant of others: he was casting doubt upon man's ability to grasp the real essence of those objects. It was this challenge to tradition that disturbed his contemporaries' (Yolton 1993: 131).

What disturbed Locke's contemporaries is what today is taken for granted, at one level of analysis at least, certainly when it comes to religious claims about the world. Yet the challenge of the temporal and the empirical that Locke posed to the tradition of his time is no different from the challenge that anyone after Locke posed to any tradition claiming to have access to timeless truths. And it is no different in this broad sense from the challenge that Derrida himself poses to the metaphysics of presence, to claims of being able to make all sorts of essences

(a) present – gift, time, truth, justice, democracy, and so on. The challenge of the temporal and the empirical is the essence of critique.

Let us note here that although Locke's arguments disturbed his contemporaries deeply, he had done much to avoid disturbing them. In particular, he had tried to diffuse concern about 'man's' utter ignorance of the essence of things by appealing to both the scriptures and common sense. Our capacity, extremely limited as it is, is nonetheless 'suited to our state and concerns' – such was Locke's main message, which he thought would reassure his readers. 'Men have reason to be well satisfied with what God hath thought fit for them, since he has given them (as St Peter says) ... whatsoever is necessary for the conveniences of life, and information of virtue.' Their hands may not be 'big enough to grasp everything', but they are still filled with 'blessings'; they may not have 'broad sunshine' to work with, but 'the candle, that is set up in us, shines bright enough for all our purposes'; they may not have 'wings to fly', but is this good enough a reason to 'sit still and perish' when they can make use of their legs (1997: 57)?

> 'Tis of great use to the sailor to know the length of his line, though he cannot with it fathom all the depths of the ocean. 'Tis well he knows that it is long enough to reach the bottom, at such places, as are necessary to direct his voyage, and caution him against running upon shoals, that may ruin him. Our business here is not to know all things, but those which concern our conduct. If we can find those measures, whereby ... ['man'] in this world, may, and ought to govern his opinions and actions depending thereon, we need not be troubled, that some other things escape our knowledge (1997: 58).

Despite Locke's colourful metaphors, his contemporaries were deeply troubled by his doctrine and remained unconvinced – as troubled and unconvinced, one might say, as Derrida's own critics are today. Although obviously Locke's time and our time are not the same, the parallel is not uncalled for. Both Locke and Derrida have been accused of precisely the same thing – epistemological and ethical relativism. And they have been accused of the same thing for the very same reason – their antiessentialism or antifoundationalism, for positing the permanent absence of essence, foundation and origin, for insisting, in short, on the inevitability of the economy of thought.

From the perspective of the religious paradigm of his time, not to mention the common sense recognition of human finitude, Locke's contention that 'our business here is not to know everything' seems, at first sight at least, quite unobjectionable. Yet, as we have seen, Locke's claim was not that man knows some things about the world and is ignorant of others. It was something far more profound and fundamental than that, namely, and to use his own metaphor, that what 'man' knows and can know is merely the surface of the ocean, not its depth. Although it is true that the sailor does not need to know the depths of the ocean to navigate, the point for his contemporaries was that he can never be certain of what he knows of the surface unless he also has knowledge of the depths. This is the deeper implication of Locke's argument, which he may or may not have understood or, at least, fully appreciated. And this is precisely the point on which his critics focused and made the main target of their attack. For the critics the issue was not necessarily how much about the world 'man' can know but rather whether he can know what can be known with any degree of certainty. As far as they were concerned, and not without good reason, Locke's argument was that certainty is not 'to be had'. Not only does Locke say so explicitly – '[we should not] require demonstration, and demand certainty, where probability only is to be had' (1997: 57) – but his entire argument points in this direction. Yolton divides the critiques of Locke's *Essay* into those concerned with epistemological scepticism and those concerned with religious and ethical scepticism, although, as he notes, the former are never completely divorced from the latter. We shall not consider these critiques here. We shall simply note that they were concerned with the two foundations of knowledge that Locke's *Essay* undermined: innate ideas and the ability of 'man' to know the essence of things. The critics' fear – critics like 'Lee and Sergeant in England and Leibniz on the Continent' (Yolton 1993: 73) – was that with these pillars removed, there was nothing to prevent thought from sliding into epistemological and ethical relativism. History was to prove Locke's critics right. Although there have been repeated attempts to arrest and neutralise relativism, the inaugural and most notable perhaps being Kant's own attempt, none of them has been successful.

Let us, then, turn to Kant and his discussion of the economy of thought as limitation to what can be grasped, which I will approach through a comparison between his critique of pure reason and Derrida's critique of the pure gift. As I noted in the last chapter, Derrida acknowledges the similarities between the two critiques. In his discussion of the gift, he notes that there is a gap between the gift and its phenomenon, the gift itself and what people in everyday life consider as gifts. His whole point is that this gap is routinely disregarded in European thought so that the gift is confused with its phenomenon, what is permanently absent assumed to be (a) present and within grasp. 'The gift *itself*', says Derrida, 'will never be confused with the presence of its phenomenon'. It ought not to be confused and perhaps will not be confused after the work of deconstruction is carried out, after it has been shown, that is, that the gap between phantom and phenomenon is irreducible. Let us note here that between the first and the second part of this sentence, Derrida introduces a clause that qualifies the 'itself' which he himself highlights. Derrida uses the expression 'the gift itself' because he does not 'dare' to use the expression 'the gift in itself', which is what his argument is pointing at: 'The gift *itself*—we dare not say the gift *in it-self*—will never be confused. ...' (1994: 29). What Derrida does not dare to say but says nonetheless, already puts us on the road that leads back to Kant and the fundamental distinction between phenomena and things in themselves – and no doubt also back to Locke himself and his distinction between nominal and real essences. Much like Kant and Locke before him, Derrida posits a fundamental and irreducible difference between the phenomenon and the thing itself (or in itself). We may even say that his critique of the pure gift reproduces the basic moves that Kant makes in his critique of pure reason. Derrida readily admits to this himself, even though he is also quick to point out that his critique is not a simple reproduction of Kant's own critique. Nonetheless, he is implicated in it, he says. We should therefore examine the extent of his involvement.

The first thing to note here is that what Derrida does in his critique of the pure gift and more broadly the critique of the 'metaphysics of presence' over and above what Kant did in his critique of pure reason does not affect the basic structure of the Kantian logic. It amplifies it, strives to make it more consistent with itself, radicalises it, takes it to its logical conclusion. If Derrida does not dare to use the Kantian term 'in it-self', it is not because he disagrees with what this notion attempts to convey – 'something, we know not what'. Rather it is because he wishes to emphasise the extent of everyone's ignorance of it – the 'it' that 'there is' and 'gives' to thought to think about – such complete and utter ignorance that for Derrida it is inappropriate to even name this 'it'. This rhetorical gesture aside, Derrida is no more able to speak about it without giving it a name than Kant ever was, even if what he has to say about it, like Kant, is that it cannot be an object of possible experience: 'It would thus be necessary to think a thing, something that would be Being and time but would not be either a being or a temporal thing' (Derrida 1994: 20).

Be that as it may, and to press on with the comparison, the gap between gift and economy, which is to say, between the phantom and the phenomenon, is nowhere to be found in the empirical world. It is a 'transcendental illusion', says Derrida, employing Kant's terminology without hesitation this time (1994: 29). This gap, he goes on to say, is 'analogous to Kant's transcendental dialectic, as relation between thinking and knowing, the noumenal and the phenomenal' (Derrida 1994: 30). It is analogous but not quite the same. Thinking this transcendental illusion, Derrida points out, is not a question of 'a simple reproduction of Kant's critical machinery. But neither is it a matter of rejecting that machinery as old fashioned. In any case, we are implicated in it....' (1994: 30). Even if one wanted to reject Kant's critical machinery, it would not be an easy because one is already caught up in it. And in any case, Derrida is not at all thinking of rejecting it. It may be old, more than two centuries old, but it is not old-fashioned. Whatever the problems with this machinery, it still works and has its uses, the most fundamental being that it can still make a sharp, deep, clean cut between the empirical and the transcendental, the phenomenon and the thing itself (or in itself). It is this division that made it possible for Kant to demonstrate the illusions of pure reason. And it is this, too, that made it possible for Derrida to demonstrate the illusion of the pure gift/present, to produce something like a critique of 'the metaphysics of presence'. If there is no pure reason to grasp things in themselves, there can be no pure gift and no pure gift of thought either. Time, being in time, in the empirical world makes them impossible.

We have been arguing that it is the metaphysics of absence that unites Kant and Derrida – the positing of the thing in itself that will never be grasped, hence never given or taken and of the present/gift itself that is also never grasped, hence never given or taken either. Yet this metaphysics divides them as well, certainly when it comes to the question of how consistently and persistently it is upheld and applied. We have already noted, and will return to this issue below, that although Kant denies the possibility of pure reason in his epistemology, at another level or in other contexts he asserts it, nowhere more so than when it comes to positing a subject that thinks for itself. Derrida by contrast has been far more meticulous in dealing with absence, more vigilant about slips of this sort. Derridarian notions like *trace* and *différance* and antics like putting words like *Being* 'under erasure' can be read as so many precautions in this respect. Here, I will provide one example that mentions Kant by name and what in his 'critical machinery' Derrida considers to be not so critical after all, not vigilant enough, perhaps even careless. The discussion is about the presumed triumph of democracy after the collapse of the Soviet Union and what some hailed as the end of history:

> It would be too easy to show that, measured by the failure to establish liberal democracy, the gap between fact and ideal essence does not show up only in these so-called primitive forms of government, theocracy and military dictatorship.... This failure and this gap also characterize, *a priori* ... *all* democracies, including the oldest and most stable of so-called Western democracies. At stake here is the very concept of democracy as concept of a promise that can only arise in such a *diastema*.... That is why we always propose to speak of a democracy *to come*, not of a *future* democracy in the future present, not even of a regulating idea, in the Kantian sense (Derrida 2006: 80–81).

As is well known, Kant allowed for a positive function for the metaphysical – a regulative function. As he argues in the 'Appendix to the Transcendental Dialectic', although metaphysical ideas are a '*focus imaginarius*—i.e., a point from which the concepts of the understanding do not really proceed, since it lies entirely outside the bounds of possible experience—nonetheless still serve to obtain for these concepts the greatest unity alongside the greatest extension'. Although outside the knowledge production-possibility boundary, they can still be useful to knowledge, provided that one is careful in dealing with them. For, as Kant goes on to say immediately, 'it is from this that there arises the deception [that these figments of the imagination are real beings]; yet this illusion ... can be prevented from deceiving' (1999: 591). Derrida is not so optimistic – and with good reason. Western thought is a prime example of this sort of self-deception. It is because of the ease with which the *focus imaginarius* is presented as a real focal point that

Derrida refuses to speak of democracy (Being, time, the gift, justice, and so on) as regulative concepts. The only thing he will allow is the expression 'democracy to come'. Unlike 'future democracy' which suggests that it will appear and become (a) present at some point in the future, 'democracy to come' is meant to say that it will never come. The instant it will come and become present, it will instantly slip into the past and disappear.

Derrida rightly considers himself among those few who have 'ceaselessly proceeded in a hyper-critical fashion ... in a deconstructive fashion' (2006: 113). And he no doubt was right to have proceeded as he did because, as history suggests, it is quite easy to mistake imagination for reality. The old lights, as we have said, were not immune to it themselves, despite the fact that it was they who drew the boundary between the two to begin with. But there is also a positive function to Derrida's own critique, and here things become more complicated. He proceeded hypercritically, he says in the same sentence, 'in the name of a *new Enlightenment* for *the century to come*' (2006: 113; my emphases). I have highlighted these expressions because they seem to me to be fraught with difficulties. A new Enlightenment presupposes an old Enlightenment, and this concept raises the inevitable question as to the use of the new. If one is already enlightened, one is already enlightened. The obvious answer to this, of course, is that one may not have been enlightened enough, that more light is needed. Is it certain however, that more is what it says it is – more? Is it beyond doubt that more is not less and reciprocally that less is less and not more? I will return to this important question in the last chapter and discuss it in greater detail. For what is at stake is precisely the possibility of enlightenment itself. The second expression – 'the century to come' – is also problematic. It is not clear whether Derrida is using the locution *to come* as he used it in the case of democracy. If he is not, he ought to. For there is no such thing as a century that will come and become present, and Derrida knows this only too well. It has been known for a very long time. As we have seen, Saint Augustine knew it and agonised over it. Yet if the century to come will never come – because at any given point in time part of it will still be in the future and part of it already in the past so that what will linger for an instant will not be century, not itself as itself – if it will not come then, what is the use of a new Enlightenment, assuming that it is possible? Is this not another way of saying that it is not possible?

'Think for Yourself'

We have already noted that Derrida's discussion of the gift as economy in the sense of exchange, circulation, and, hence, circularity presupposes the existence of the economy of thought as a limitation to what can be known. It is because, to use Locke's metaphor, 'man's' hands are not big enough to grasp the essence of things that what he gives is not of the essence, not a true gift but a semblance of the gift, its phenomenon. It is because he grasps things in time or in the meantime and not instantly, not in the present, that he cannot give and keep a present, that what he gives always already comes back and what he takes is always already given back.

We have also noted that Locke and Kant were not unaware of the existence of an economy of thought in this sense, even if, one has to assume, whatever understanding of it they may have had could not have derived from their epistemological writings. For the way in which they portrayed this economy contradicts the other – the economy of thought as limitation to what can be grasped – which they themselves posited. In saying that the subject ought to think for itself, Locke and Kant at once sketched the economy of thought as a circle and erased it. Or, they sketched it as a partial rather than a general economy, one that excludes the thinking subject because this subject is said to be capable of giving to itself (gifts of thought) – a case of mistaking the phantom for a real thing. As we have said and will try to demonstrate in what follows, if there is no gift, there is no gift, whether it is given by one subject to another or by the subject to itself. My aim in this section is simply to highlight the economy of thought as a circle in Locke's and Kant's texts. I will take up the question of its limitations and exclusions in subsequent chapters.

Let us begin with a few preliminary remarks. To say that the subject ought to think for itself, as Kant says in his famous essay on enlightenment, is not to say that it should refuse to listen to what others have to say, how they themselves think about things. 'This cannot be right', says Bittner (1996: 346) in his discussion of the different possible readings of Kant's argument. 'It is neither desirable nor even attainable. We do not wish, nor are we able to do our thinking alone to the point of not even considering others' views.' What Kant meant to say, Bittner goes on to say, is that one should not act 'on the basis of somebody else's judgment, without checking its accuracy. ...' To think for oneself, then, is to refuse to take what others say 'on trust', as Locke says, as it is granted or as we would say today *for granted*, in other words, take it as a grant or gift. That one should take what others have to say seriously is only right and proper, but this taking cannot be the taking of a gift of thought – not even when what is taken happens to be true, says Locke in his own discussion. Even if it is true, it is still not the truth, and will not become so unless and until the thinking subject decides for itself and by itself that it is the truth, authorises it as such, puts its stamp of approval on it.

For the Enlightenment, then – if by this term we understand what Kant says we ought to understand – there can be no gift of thought even when what is given is a gift of thought – the truth. To take things for granted is to give – and it is to give far more than what one takes. As we have already noted, it is to give in to the giver and hence give up the most valuable of all of one's assets, namely, one's autonomy. And the other way round. As we shall see, for both Locke and Kant giving is taking, an investment that generates profit, namely, the power that one acquires and exercises over those that one makes dependent. The assumption that there is no gift of thought in the sense we have just described is fundamental. Take this assumption away and the Enlightenment collapses. It becomes unenlightened, unreasonable, uneconomical, counterproductive. For why waste time and energy to think for yourself, to reinvent the wheel over and over again, when it has already been invented and can be used by anyone who wishes to use it?

We will turn first to Locke, who wastes not time in making an issue of this circular economy, even if it is not until the end of book I of the *Essay* that he lays his cards open and spells out why 'men must think and know for themselves' (1997: 105). From the very beginning of the *Essay*, even before the beginning in 'The Epistle to the Reader', we already encounter a description of what happens when one does not think for oneself. 'He who has raised himself above the alms-basket', Locke says to the reader, 'and not content to live *lazily* on scraps of begged opinions, sets his own thoughts on work, to find and follow truth' (1997: 7). I have highlighted the term *lazily* for future reference. We will encounter the same sort of explanation as to why 'men' do not think for themselves in Kant, and we will contrast it with the sociologically grounded explanation that the social sciences developed. For the moment, let us stay with the colourful picture that Locke sketches in this short extract. For all we know, he may be describing an everyday scene from late-seventeenth-century London, only that the beggar sitting at the corner is not a man who does not make use of his hands but a man who does not make use of his understanding. The metaphor of begging for food (for thought), the image of the alms basket, of subsisting on scraps that one has begged for, the need to raise oneself above such a condition – apparently unworthy of a human being – all this points to what we have been saying: that to take is to give and to take without making a return of equivalent value is to give far more than what one takes. As we have seen in the brief discussion on Mauss in the last chapter, it is to lose face forever, to face subordination, to become a client and subservient or minister – a term etymological linked to the idea of being a minor, which we will also encounter in Kant. Locke's picture of the 'man' who does not think for himself is painted in even darker colours, no doubt for maximum effect. He is not referring to someone who is at least keeping up the pretence of still being in the game of giving and taking, as Mauss does. It is clear that Locke's 'man' has given up on giving completely and is content to live by taking. And because he only takes, he has given up everything.

Towards the end of first book of the *Essay*, Locke will make his stronger case yet for the impossibility of a gift of thought. It is in these last sections of the book also that, as we shall see shortly, he completes his sketch of this circular economy by focusing on the other half of the circle – giving – and how it is that it is also taking. The discussion is about the search for truth and the imperative of using 'our own thoughts, than other men's to find it'. What follows is what we have come to expect from Locke – another colourful metaphor. If it is irrational to expect that one can see with someone else's eyes, it is as irrational to expect that one can know through someone else's understanding, to see through the mind's eye of another. It is the subject's own eyes that are the source of all vision and its own mind that is the source of all knowledge and truth. We will encounter the same sort of argument in Kant, who will posit the subject's reason as the 'supreme touchstone of truth', the origin of all legitimate signification. But what if, one might ask, that which another 'man' sees happens to be true, a true vision of the world? Would that not make it true also for every other 'man', a real gift of thought? Not so, according to Locke. Each 'man' must see the truth through his own eyes. Until then, what is true will not be true:

> For, I think, we may as rationally hope to see with other men's eyes, as to know by other men's understandings.... The floating of other men's opinions in our brains, makes us not one jot the more knowing, though they happen to be true. What in them was science, is in us but opiniatrety.... Such borrowed wealth, like fairy-money, though it were gold in the hand from which he received it, will be but leaves and dust when it comes to use (Locke 1997: 105).

There is no gift of thought then, not even when what is given is science, gold, the truth itself. As soon as it changes hands it is ontologically transformed and becomes something entirely different: mere opinion, fairy-money, leaves that crumble into dust. It becomes a phantom because the subject that takes it without thinking for itself does not know its value, what it is, what it does, or how it is to be used. It becomes mere opinion, repeating without knowing, taking without having, because nothing is really taken – not taken in, not grasped or understood, hence not in one's possession. We may say, putting words in Locke's mouth, that although the subject takes it, it does not really get it.

Let us note a few things about Locke's argument, first, the circularity in which the subject is involved. Although the gift may be gold it would have no value until the subject recognises its value by itself, which is to say, in a tautological sort of way, that the subject would not know its value until it knows it. Let us also note that the argument of vision is itself flawed. In a certain sense, not a physical sense to be sure, there is nothing that the subject sees through its own eyes. If it sees and recognises what it sees, that is, recognises it as worth seeing, as something relevant and meaningful, it is only because it has been taught that it is relevant and meaningful. In this sense, it always sees with another 'man's' eyes – what its culture makes visible.

In the penultimate section of the first book of the *Essay* Locke reiterates his view of how 'men' come to believe in the existence of innate ideas and principles. It is a question of logical conformity, he suggests. Once 'men' realised that certain principles could not be doubted, they concluded that they were innate. Yet this was not the only reason. 'Men' were also discouraged from thinking about them in any other way, discouraged from thinking for themselves. 'It was no small advantage to those who affected to be masters and teachers, to make this the principle of *principles,* that principles must not be questioned.' And so, says Locke – assuming what has been the dominant assumption for a very long time, namely, that consent is a matter of persuasion at the discursive level, making others see and believe through the sheer force of rational argumentation – and so, he says, they believed and took these principles 'upon trust, without further examination'. Such was the state to which 'men' were reduced, a 'posture of blind credulity' in which:

> they might be more easily governed by, and made useful to some sort of men, who had the skill and office to principle and guide them. Nor is it a small power it gives one man over another, to have the authority to be the dictator of principles, and teacher of unquestionable truths; and to make a man swallow that for an innate principle, which may serve to his purpose, who teacheth them (Locke 1997: 106).

With this, the circle of the circular economy of thought closes. If to take is to give – to give in and to give up to the extent that one becomes a client or, worse, a beggar – it is equally the case that to give is to take. Giving what passes as a gift of thought, as unquestionable truths, pays, and pays handsomely – such is Locke's argument. It pays those who give with what it takes away from those who take – the authority to dictate and the power to teach.

Locke's encouragement to the credulous and the ignorant to think for themselves does not seem to have been well received in certain circles. In a letter to Locke one of his close friends spells out the reasons:

> I fancy I pretty well guess what it is that some men find mischievous in your *Essay*: it is opening the eyes of the ignorant, and rectifying the methods of reasoning, which perhaps may undermine some received errors, and so abridge the empire of darkness; wherein, though the subjects wonder deplorably, *yet the rulers have their profit and advantage* [my emphasis].[4]

Let us now turn to Kant and his celebrated essay 'An Answer to the Question: What is Enlightenment?' As we have already noted, for Kant the essence of enlightenment is the willingness of the subject to think for itself, to use its own understanding rather than the understanding of another: '*Enlightenment is man's emergence from his self-incurred immaturity. Immaturity* is the inability to use one's own understanding without the guidance of another' (1991a [1784]: 54). I shall explore here briefly the moves with which Kant sketches the economy of thought as a circle, the understanding in other words that giving is taking and taking giving. At one level of analysis this economy is explicit in what Kant has to say on the surface of his text, so much so in fact that it becomes almost indistinguishable from the market economy. If one does not wish to use one's own understanding and relies on someone else to get things done, one has to pay. It may be convenient, but convenience comes at a price:

> It is so convenient to be immature! If I have a book to have understanding in place of me, a spiritual adviser to have a conscience for me, a doctor to judge my diet for me, and so on, I need not make any efforts at all. I need not think so long as I can pay; others will soon enough take the tiresome job over for me (1991a: 54).

In this extract Kant portrays the immature almost as a consumer. Because one can afford to pay for the services of others, one does not need to bother about thinking for oneself. As things are presented here then, there is nothing much if anything at all to distinguish the economy of thought from the market economy. If nothing is free in the market, nothing is free in the economy of thought either. In both there is a price to pay for taking, which is to say, as we have been saying, in both taking is at the same time giving. As we shall see in the last chapter, Kant has in fact been read as saying that there is no difference between the two economies. And this led to the obvious objection: we cannot do all the thinking that needs to be done by ourselves, the same way that we cannot (any longer) produce everything we consume by ourselves. Moreover, even if we could, it would be totally inefficient and counterproductive, an irrational and unenlightened way of doing things, as we have noted. If there is anything that the market economy teaches us, this is the benefits of the division of labour.

As we have said this reading stays at the surface of Kant's text. There is a difference between the market economy and the economy of thought and a fundamental one at that. The former does not pretend to be anything other than economy; the latter is an economy in denial. Everyone presumes that when it comes to knowledge, what is given by one subject to another – by the scholar or the clergyman, let us say, to the community – is a gift, not something for which one must pay. Kant's whole point is precisely to show that it is an economy, that whoever takes (for granted) will have to pay a price and a high one at that – nothing less than one's autonomy. It is because of this cost that Kant considers those who pay it, not only lazy but also cowards: 'Laziness and cowardice are the reasons why such a large proportion of men ... remain immature for life' (1991: 54). It takes courage to use one's own understanding, audacity to become free, an idea that Kant turned into the motto of enlightenment: *sapere aude*. Instead of taking responsibility for themselves, most 'men' – not to mention women – choose to hide behind someone else, a guardian who thinks and speaks on their behalf as though they were still minors. The image becomes darker as the text unfolds. Such people become 'domesticated animals', 'docile creatures' tied onto a 'leading-string' – all metaphors that, as we shall see, Kant uses to highlight what one gives (up) when one takes (for granted) what is not a gift.

The theme of losing one's autonomy in this way has been repeated countless of times since Locke's and Kant's time. Of all the examples that one could use,

I have chosen one in which this lesson was given (as a gift no doubt) at a university, for this locus of the universal is something that I wish to return to. It is Max Weber's famous essay on 'Science as a Vocation' – originally a speech, say the editors of the text, at Munich University delivered in 1918 (1958:129). The discussion is on the 'disenchantment of the world' and the consequent meaninglessness as the fate of the times:

> To the person who cannot bear the fate of the times *like a man*, one must say: may he rather return silently.... The arms of the old churches are open widely and compassionately for him. After all, they do not make it hard for him. One way or another he has to bring his 'intellectual sacrifice'—that is inevitable. If he can really do it, we shall not rebuke him (1958: 155; my emphases).

We shall not rebuke any 'man' who sacrifices his intellectual freedom for the safety provided by religion, says Weber, but he is only saying that we will not. He is being rhetorical. He has already rebuked this 'man', and severely so. He has said from the very beginning and in no uncertain terms that he is a coward – not 'man' enough to bear the fate of the times.

If the economy of thought – which Kant is presupposing in his plea to the subject to think for itself – is truly a circle, the terms of exchange must be reversible. If taking is giving – giving in to the guardians and, hence, giving up one's autonomy – one should also expect giving to be taking. The latter aspect of the circularity is implicit in Kant's depiction of the figure of the guardian. 'Having first infatuated their domesticated animals, and carefully prevented the docile creatures from daring to take a single step without the leading-strings to which they are tied', Kant says, 'they next show them the danger which threatens them if they try to walk unaided' (1991a: 54). It pays to give, Kant is suggesting in this passage. The reward or return is the power that one exercises over those whom one has domesticated, which, as Locke reminds us in his own discussion, is 'no small power'. And because it does pay and is profitable, the charisma or rhetoric that first infatuates and the care that prevents from moving on to other pastures is followed by a demonstration of the dangers that threaten such a move. The guardians, Kant is suggesting in this extract, work hard to keep their docile creatures on the leash, to prevent them from thinking for themselves and becoming what they ought to be – free. And although their labour is unacceptable and should be severely criticised – it constitutes nothing less than a 'crime against human nature', says Kant (1991a: 57) – it is nonetheless understandable, at least from the point of view of economic rationality. No one likes to lose a good customer, whether in the market economy or in the economy of thought.

There is no gift of thought for the Enlightenment then, only a circular economy in which giving is taking and taking giving. And because there is no gift, because taking (for granted) is giving (in and up), the subject must think for itself at all times. If it is to avoid subjection it must become thoroughly subjective, which is to say, constitute itself as the origin of all value and the source of all truth. '*To think for oneself* means to look within oneself (i.e. in one's own reason) for the supreme touchstone of truth; and the maxim of thinking for oneself at all times is **enlightenment**' (Kant 1991b[1786]: 249, footnote; emphases in original).

It is because of autonomy that the maxim or motto of the Enlightenment has been so central in the history of European thought, why it has long been institutionalised and 'universalised'. For there is no doubt that it is the most fundamental premise of the institution that professes the universal, that domain in which reason reaches its highest summits, namely, the university. Here the subject is *taught* in a properly Kantian fashion and as a matter of course to think for itself at all times – a contradiction in terms, as we shall see shortly. It is encouraged to say what it thinks, to make up its own mind, to decide all by itself and for itself what the truth is because the 'supreme touchstone of truth' is none other than itself. It is here, in short, that the subject is taught the art of auto-giving, which is not only a fantasy but also an art of mistrust. It is in this institution too that another subject is fashioned along the very same lines – a collective subject this time. This is the subject that postcolonial scholars have been striving to provincialize – Europe or if one prefers to call it by its synonym, modernity.

Of all the examples that one could use to show how vital, fundamental, and alive the idea of modernity still is, and with it or in it the idea of enlightenment itself, I have selected one that is currently circulating widely and is highly influential. I have selected it also because it cuts through all secondary traits and associations and comes straight to the point – which is the point of the Enlightenment itself: think for yourself. It is the theory of so-called 'reflexive modernization', a pleonasm to be sure because the whole point of this theory – if that is how it should be thought of[5] – is that the essence of the modern is reflexivity. It is this bending back to look at oneself, this turning around or turning inside to look within oneself, as Kant says, which is meant to be an exercise in questioning everything that one is given or has ever taken for granted that makes the modern what it is, according to the theory. And to be sure, it is a turning around or inside exactly as Kant described it, one said to be happening at all times, one that excludes nothing from scrutiny, not even itself. 'What is characteristic of modernity', says one of its leading proponents, 'is not an embracing of the new for its own sake, but the presumption of *wholesale* reflexivity – which of course includes reflection upon the nature of reflection itself' (Giddens 1990: 39; my emphasis). Modernity could be mistaken for something that embraces the new for its own sake because it produces the new. Yet it produces it, if it does, not as end in itself but as the unintended outcome of this art of auto-giving – reflexivity. As for the other of modernity, that for the sake of which the postcolonial critic is striving to provincialize Europe even as, or rather precisely because he thinks of it as a gift, the presumption is the reverse. The other of modernity is either completely unaware of itself because it does not ever think of itself for itself as a self – modernity thinks of it as a self on its behalf – as in 'oral cultures', or if it does, its reflexivity is of the retail kind, a bit of thinking here and a bit there, as in 'premodern civilisations' (1990: 37).

In subsequent chapters we will have the opportunity to examine closely both presumptions (in the double sense of this term): the presumption about the individual subject that gives itself auto-generously and auto-nomously and the presumption about the collective subject that, having given to itself historically in this way, can now afford to give to everyone else – 'to us all', as the postcolonial critic says. Here it should suffice to make some preliminary remarks about the individual subject, and this as a means of paving the way for the discussion on the social sciences that follows.

Let us note, to begin with, what Hamann noted long time ago, soon after the publication of Kant's essay on the question of enlightenment. In a letter to a friend, Hamann, who was also Kant's friend, argued that it is not immaturity which is self-incurred, as Kant claimed in his essay, but guardianship. If there is immaturity it is because some people – apparently Kant, even though Hamann does not say so explicitly – appoint themselves by themselves as the guardians of others.[6] With this Hamann put his finger on a central paradox, even if he did not pursue its implications. Kant was obviously arguing against guardianship, but he could do so from no other position except the position of a guardian – the position of someone who took over from others the 'tiresome job' of thinking and did it on their behalf. He did so even if his aim was precisely to put an end to this practice. He had no choice in the matter. To make the argument that the subject ought to think for itself at all times, Kant had no option but to ask the subject not to think for itself, to suspend thinking for itself at least once and to take Kant's argument for granted. In short, in making this argument Kant also unmade it – and did so at the same time. Such is the paradox. Apparently Kant forgot to remember precisely what he himself had taught – that any venturing beyond the knowledge production-possibility boundary can only lead to contradictions and paradoxes. He forgot to remember that the thinking subject is as much a subject as the unthinking subject, that it too is caught up in the empirical and operates in time or in the meantime, in short, that it cannot give without taking (or take without giving).

The Socialisation of Thought

The social sciences have inherited the economy of thought from the philosophers of the Enlightenment. And it is from them also that they have inherited the belief that the subject is capable of thinking for itself, what amounts to another economy – an auto-economy – which is what the etymological sense of the term as well as the sense in which Aristotle used it points to: the household as the legislator of its own rules – auto-nomy – and as an independent producer and consumer of value – aut(o)-arky. Autonomy and autarky are also the values of the subject that presumes to think for itself, the subject that retreats to, or constructs for itself an 'inner citadel', as Berlin (1969: 135) says, and makes itself its own master behind high walls. On the one hand, then, there is the inheritance of the economy of thought as limitation to what can be grasped and as the circle in which this limitation is implicated; on the other, the inheritance of an auto-economy of auto-gifts of thought – autonomy, truth, and what is critical for the social sciences, the condition of possibility of truth, namely, objectivity.

Whether these economies are compatible, whether an auto-economy is at all possible is the fundamental question that this books raises. We have already indicated that it is not possible and noted the paradox with which it is burdened. In this section we shall turn to the social sciences and explore what happened to the inheritance of the Enlightenment. We shall examine how the economy of thought was transformed through the socialisation of thought, which is to say, its temporalization or historicization; the specific issues that arose as a result of this transformation, notably the question of objectivity; and finally, in dealing with this question, how the social sciences sought to come to terms with the contradiction we have just noted and of which they themselves became keenly aware at some point in their development: positing an economy of thought and denying it at the same time by maintaining the fiction of a persona that can step outside this economy – the subject that thinks for itself.

Let us first note that in a certain sense the economy of thought occupies a privileged position in the social sciences or, at any rate, that these sciences are predisposed to emphasising the limits of thought and the circle in which these limits are implicated – which is not to say that they practice what they preach. Historically their key premises were forged in reaction to philosophy and its perceived tendency to give thought free reign – what Bourdieu (2000: 27) more recently called referring to Heidegger as a paradigmatic example of this tendency, 'the hubris of thought without limits'. Marx is probably the key figure here, having turned Hegel on his head, as it is often said, by insisting on the primacy of life over consciousness. But no less important is Durkheim's social epistemology and the primacy he accorded to the social life of the group and the collective representations that develop from it over the consciousness of the individual. If anything, Durkheim was even more radical than Marx in socialising thought. Having swept away both empiricism and rationalism with a wave of the hand, he was to argue that even the categories of the understanding that Kant posited as a priori, as a given (gift of nature), were the product of society – which, let us note here in passing, was one of the claims that his biographer was to call Durkheim's sociological imperialism (Lukes 1973).

Let us note also the outline of the economy of thought as exchange or circle, the giving that is also taking and the taking that is also giving. The paradigmatic figure once again is Marx, who, much like the philosophers of the Enlightenment, sketched the exchange in political rather than epistemological terms. The key notion here is ideology, its giving that is also a taking from the proletariat and its taking that is also a giving in to the bourgeoisie. But the presence of the circle is not restricted to Marx's work. Another strand, equally important, can be traced in Durkheim's own work. Here giving and taking is implicit in Durkheim's view of the symbolic, which, much like ideology, is understood as covering up the real underneath. There is cost for taking the symbolic for granted, a cost for society to begin with, which condemns itself in this way to an 'elementary form' of life, and a cost also that the individual pays, even as it has not been born yet, precisely because it is prevented by the circumstances from being born. Although their political orientations are different, these two strands converge on a point that is of interest to us in this investigation and to which we shall return in the next chapter. It is the idea of making one's own history, of penetrating the historical unconscious – what society takes for granted – making it conscious and bringing it under rational control.

The concern with liberation is not new, of course. Nor is the posing of the question of knowledge with an eye on the question of power new, however furtive or unfocused the glance might have been earlier. We have traced this concern as far back as Locke and his *Essay*, which, as we have seen, was found by his contemporaries to be highly disturbing for having opened 'the eyes of the ignorant' and turned them again their rulers who had, at their expense, 'their profit and advantage'. What is new, to the extent that anything can be, is the positing of the social as both that which sets limits to thought and explains subjection to the powers that be. As Bauman (2000: 17) noted recently, the question of liberation emerges as a problem once a 'distinction between "objective" and "subjective" freedom' has been made. No doubt. But it is a problem posed in very different terms from those of the philosophers of the Enlightenment. Taking for granted, hence giving in and giving up, is no longer a question of laziness or cowardice. It is now seen as the outcome of a profound misunderstanding of the nature of social reality, the misapprehension of the social as something natural and necessary hence also immutable – whether this misunderstanding is said to be the result of an orchestrated misrepresentation by the powers that be, as in the case of ideology, or the result of the circularity through which the social is experienced, which is what the notion of hegemony is meant to convey. We will return to these ideas in the next chapter, in which we will discuss in detail the question of liberation. My concern here is with the other gift of thought that thinking for oneself is said to make possible – truth and its condition of possibility, namely, objectivity. We will turn first to how the economy of thought appears in the social sciences from this epistemic angle.

To put it schematically and simplify what is no doubt a complex picture, limitation in social science with regard to what can be grasped and hence given (phenomena) consists of what is referred to, often interchangeably as the social, cultural, or historical positioning and conditioning of the subject. We shall keep these aspects analytically distinct as they refer to the conditioning of the subject by different sets of conditions: the conditions of a social group within a particular society, of one society in relation to another, and of a specific historical period in relation to other historical periods, respectively. But we shall also move beyond these distinctions and the spatial metaphor that makes them possible because what is of essence here and what unifies them at a higher level of analysis is not space but time. We are referring to time as the temporality of the subject, the fact that it grasps, not time itself or, what is another way of saying the same thing, not in an instant, but *in* time. This is, in the first instance, the time it takes for anyone to become a subject that grasps and acts and what in the meantime the subject takes to become subject – the values, norms, and ideas of one's social group, culture, and historical period. It is a question of being a finite being, no doubt, a finitude that reflects the denaturalization, hence temporalization of the subject that, as we have seen, was initiated by Locke who cut off the subject from the timeless truths imprinted on its mind by God and blocked in this way the possibility of instantaneous recognition and understanding.

The dependence of the subject on the social that the social sciences introduced, which is an elaboration of the dependence on the empirical that the philosophers of the Enlightenment postulated, was anticipated by Hamann, Kant's contemporary and friend, in his 'Metacritique' of Kant's *Critique of Pure Reason*. Hamann's argument was that even though Kant placed limits to what reason can grasp and demonstrated that it cannot be pure, he nonetheless preserved its purity in another way – by bracketing off the thinking subject from the social as though it did its thinking in a void. As Hamann put it, Kant made reason 'independent of all tradition and custom and belief in them' as well as the means through which tradition and custom are transmitted, namely, language (1996b [1800]: 155). As we have already noted, this dependence on the social was by all accounts first posited by Marx and was further elaborated by Durkheim in his social epistemology, even if both were to follow in Kant's steps and preserve the purity of reason by postulating a subject that could become independent by thinking for itself. As we shall see shortly, it was even acknowledged by Weber himself, who is often presumed to be in the opposite camp in this respect. It was acknowledged, in fact, in a way that implicated the scholastic subject itself and raised for the first time, at least in the social sciences, the thorny question of whether the subject in general and the scholastic subject in particular can ever think for itself. Any rate, the point to be made at this stage of the argument is that for all three ('founding fathers'), the subject is no longer the lone thinking machine confronting the empirical world and making sense of it through this encounter, whether from scratch and without any tools – as 'white paper' – or armed with the a priori gifts of nature that Kant posited. It is decisively situated in a preexisting tradition, a system of values, beliefs, and thought patterns and entangled in the language it has inherited.

This is probably the most fundamental premise of the social sciences, certainly of social epistemology if not of a sociology of knowledge. For even though the latter was announced in the nineteenth century and was developed by Mannheim by the early decades of the twentieth, it was never destined to become a sociological specialisation or, at any rate, not destined to occupy a place in the limelight. I have already noted some of the reasons for this failure, first and foremost the fact that it undermines the assumption or presumption of a subject capable of thinking for itself, of giving itself gifts of thought without having to take beforehand, and, hence, without having to give (in and up) as a result. It makes such as subject impossible, a figment of the imagination, first and foremost a figment of the scholastic subject's imagination because it is primarily this subject that entertains illusions of this sort. Let us note here briefly how a watered-down version of this specialisation – sociology of knowledge – deals with the legitimate question of how those who make it their business to show how people in everyday life know come themselves to know things. 'To include epistemological questions concerning the validity of sociological knowledge in the sociology of knowledge is somewhat like trying to push a bus in which one is riding.... We therefore exclude [them]' (Berger and Luckmann 1971: 25). 'We exclude' epistemological questions when it comes to epistemology itself, one is tempted to add, and we continue riding the bus happily pretending that it is going somewhere and will reach some destination, when in fact it is only going round and round in circles. We exclude such questions because we do not wish to acknowledge that we are caught in a circle with no means of escape.

The subject of the social sciences then, is in theory at least the polar opposite of the Kantian subject – the subject whose reason is independent of tradition, custom, and language and can therefore think for itself by means of its (pure) reason alone. '*Strictly* speaking', says Mannheim, 'it is incorrect to say that the single individual thinks':

> Rather it is more correct to insist that it participates in thinking further what other men have thought before him. He finds himself in an inherited situation with patterns of thought which are appropriate to his situation and attempts to elaborate further the inherited modes of response or to substitute others for them in order to deal more adequately with the new challenges which have arisen out of *shifts and changes* in his situation. Every individual is therefore in a two-fold sense predetermined by the fact of growing up in a society: on the one hand he finds a ready-made situation and on the other he finds in that situation performed patterns of thought and of conduct (Mannheim 1936: 2–3).

For the social sciences or, at any rate, for a social science based on a robust and consistent social epistemology, strictly speaking, the subject finds nothing within itself, certainly not the ideas that it uses to think with and not the values that make these ideas relevant and meaningful and imbue them with motivational force. Whatever it finds, it has inherited. Hence, the limitation with respect to what it can grasp (and therefore give). To put it in the more familiar spatial terms, what the subject grasps is what appears from the particular social, cultural, and historical position it happens to occupy, the angle of vision that this position makes possible – which is its inheritance. No doubt the subject can change its position and look at the world from another angle, hence see it in another light. It can disinherit itself. One thing it can never do, however, the most fundamental, is to be without any inheritance at all, to occupy no position at all, to be nowhere or everywhere, to step outside the world and look it in its totality, grasp it with one glance in an instant and know what and how it truly is. No matter how hard it tries, it will always find itself anchored somewhere, occupying a particular position, hence always seeing things as they appear from where it stands. No matter how hard it tries, what it will ever be able to grasp are phenomena, not things as they are in themselves. If the Kantian subject was burdened by a nature it could not change, the subject of social science is burdened with a sociality and historicity from which it cannot escape.

All this is well known, of course, and we have reiterated it here only to highlight the limitation to what the subject of the social sciences is able to grasp, the knowledge production-possibility boundary. Let us now turn to the circle in which this limitation is implicated. We will broach it through the familiar claim that knowledge is partial. Among the meanings attached to this term is the meaning of being incomplete, and one could therefore say that if knowledge is partial, it is because there are still things to be added to it. Yet both the dictionary definition and the way the term is used in the social sciences points to another range of meanings. Knowledge is partial also because it is subjective, or biased, or *interested*. We will capitalise on this last term and strain to hear what it says. To be interested is obviously to be concerned with, attentive to, attracted by something. It is to believe that this something has significance and value, that it makes some kind of a difference. This is consistent with the literal meaning of interest – to be or rest in between – which could be read as creating or making a difference where previously there was none, in other words, differentiating and identifying things (which are of interest). As we shall see, this reading is compatible with the widespread understanding that it is the subject that invests the world with significance, that insofar as it is not disinterested and indifferent to the world, it is because it creates all those differences in it that for the subject make a difference. To be interested, then, is to have a stake in the creation of something – in this case a *stake* in the production and dissemination of knowledge, hence the related meaning of interest as benefit, advantage, or gain, which is what the expression 'interested knowledge' is pointing to.

If knowledge is interested therefore, it is precisely because it pays some kind of an interest – the profits of recognition, for example, and whatever material benefits come with recognition. If it is interested, it is because giving knowledge (as a gift of thought) is at the same time a taking – taking something in return and with a certain capitalisation, namely, the interest. To say this is not to suggest that the subject strives to know and to disseminate what it knows to serve its personal interests. We are long past such a narrow, not to say vulgar, understanding of what the epistemic subject does. What it does, as a matter of course at any rate, is the contrary. As we have noted in the last chapter, what this subject wishes above anything else is to give, not to take. It desires to give everything, even if everything does not necessarily mean knowledge of everything, even if it only means everything there is to know about a particular aspect of the social. The problem with giving gifts of thought or, to be more precise, the problem with being unable to give them as gifts has less to do with ulterior motives than with the circularity of the circle or, what is another way of saying the same thing, the subjectivism of the subject. As soon as the epistemic subject gives, it takes. Something always returns – and returns instantly – even if what returns is only confirmation of the subject's identity as such-and-such person, the pleasure of knowing that one is doing the right thing, fighting the good battle, doing something useful, and so on. As soon as the subject reflects, long before it even considers the possibility of making its reflections public – as a public good, for the taking – something is instantly reflected in the reflection. It takes no time at all for this something to be reflected in the reflection because, as we have said, the subject has already taken and lives on *borrowed* time – the time it takes anyone to become a subject. What is reflected in the reflection is nothing other than its positioning and conditioning, its commitment to certain ideas, ideals, and values, the investments it has made in life. What is reflected, in short, is nothing other than the subject itself. Although it talks about everything except itself, it says nothing that does not refer back to itself, nothing that does not return to confirm it as the subject that it is.

This theorisation gives the motto of the Enlightenment a different spin and sets a different task for the subject that wishes to think for itself. Thinking for oneself can no longer simply be a question of refusing to take for granted the gifts of thought offered by others, and reciprocally, as we have noted, taking for granted can no longer be simply a question of laziness or cowardice. Thinking for oneself is also, more fundamentally, a refusal to take for granted what one is and, by extension, the conditions that have made one what it is. Long before the subject becomes capable of thinking for itself (if this is what it does), long before it is *taught* explicitly to refuse the gifts of thought offered by others – a contradiction in terms, as we have noted – the subject has already taken for granted and is always already indebted. This is to say that before it can begin to give itself auto-gifts of thought, the subject must first purge itself from whatever it has already taken. It must become impartial and disinterested, that is, objective. The primary task after the socialisation of thought then, is to liberate oneself from what has been taken for granted, from the collective guardian known as society.

It is to make the social, cultural, and historical unconscious conscious, to make the past present, hence, also a present to oneself. This is one of the basic differences between the philosophers of the Enlightenment and social theorists. Marx was a transitional figure in this respect. Although credited with the discovery of the social conditioning of thought, he was in many ways still thinking like Locke and Kant, hence the notion of ideology as a system of ideas taken for granted at the discursive level because a charismatic subject, let us say, persuaded another that what it says is true.

We shall not be concerned here with the different attempts to constitute an objective epistemic subject. Nor shall we be concerned with theories of objectivity. We will explore rather the current state of play and how the social sciences have reached this point in the game – a point where objectivity is increasingly thought of as a mirage. This is not to say, of course, that there is consensus on the matter – far from it. Yet although there is no consensus as such, it would probably be fair to say that in a postpositivist era and in the aftermath of poststructuralism, few would be prepared to claim access to the truth of the social or that, 'given time', the truth will eventually be grasped and social reality mapped out for everyone to see. Even fewer would be prepared to believe them. The word *truth* and related concepts such as reality have become something of a taboo. 'Uttering the word "truth" in scientific circles (like "reality", by the way) signals ignorance, mediocrity, unreflected use of ambiguous, emotion-laden words from everyday language' (Beck 1992: 166). One need not share Beck's ultimate aim – which, as Alexander (1996) says, is to turn the pathologies of modernity into virtues – to recognise that what he is describing here is a pervasive attitude premised on the finitude of the subject. Notions like truth and reality belong to everyday life and express the natural attitude towards the world, which, being unreflective, does not know any better. The practitioners of the social sciences, on the other hand, Beck is suggesting, do know better. Being a scientific circle of reflexive and rational individuals, they know that they are caught in a circle, even as they refuse to admit and accept it. And because they do know, they use terms like *truth* and *reality* with care – by placing them in quotation marks, for example – lest anyone thinks of them as ignorant and mediocre.

If we were to trace the history of this recognition of the circle (and its simultaneous denial) in the social sciences, we would have to go back to Max Weber. Unlike Marx and Durkheim, who placed themselves outside the economy of thought they themselves had posited, Weber could see no such external position. But neither could he accept the implications of the encirclement. Thus Weber would, on the one hand, argue that there can be no objectivity in the social sciences and, on the other, insist that this does not mean that scientific knowledge is subjective. We shall examine here one of Weber's most explicit statements on the issue, his essay on '"Objectivity" in Social Science and Social Policy'. Let us note to begin with that the way in which Weber distinguishes between the two disciplines already indicates that he is not about to give up on the idea of objectivity so easily. Social policy, he says, is the 'statement of ideals', social science the 'analysis of facts' (Weber 1949: 60). The former is about how things ought to be, the latter how things actually are. But it should be clear also from the title of the essay and the quotation marks around objectivity that he is not prepared to endorse it without qualifications either. 'There is no *absolutely* "objective" scientific analysis of culture', says Weber, or 'of "social phenomena" *independent* of special and "one-sided" viewpoints according to which—expressly or tacitly, consciously or unconsciously—they are selected, analyzed and organized for expository purposes' (1949 [1904]: 72; my emphases). The assumption that such analysis of culture or social phenomena is possible, Weber will go on to say, is the 'naive self-deception of the specialist who is unaware that it is due to [his] evaluative ideas ... that he has selected from an absolute infinity a tiny portion with the study of which he *concerns* himself' (1949: 82). Facts do not speak for themselves – this is Weber's key message. They do not even know that they are facts until someone – the specialist – decides that they are. They become facts only because the epistemic subject selects and analyses them. And it selects and analyses them not because they are self-evidently factual, not because they have intrinsic and universal significance that cannot be missed, but because the epistemic subject decides they have value on the basis of its own evaluative ideas, because they are relevant and meaningful to the subject in question. In short, they are facts precisely because they are subjective.

So far there is little to distinguish social science from social policy. Both appear to operate on the basis of ideals and values – not what actually is but what ought to be. But Weber will not be content to leave things at that. Having taken away the possibility of objectivity in social science with one hand, he will now try to give it back with the other. Let us note that Weber has already prepared the ground for at least a partial rehabilitation of objectivity by introducing in his text the key term *absolutely*, which I have highlighted in the quotation above: 'There is no absolutely objective scientific analysis'. There may be no absolute objectivity in scientific analysis, but this does not mean that objectivity is absolutely chimera. There can be objective analysis to a certain degree, partly objective and partly not, a more or less objective analysis, possibly and preferably more rather than less. If so, not everything is lost. Much of it goes by the board no doubt, but something still remains to hold on to. We have encountered this theme of the degree, of the more or less and the relatively several times already. It appears without fail in the writings of all those who cannot deal with the encirclement of the circle and strive to find some kind of an opening. It is the last barricade, their ultimate defensive position before the relativism that lurks in the background comes flooding in. Let us then explore here how well Weber's last barricade holds.

A few pages later Weber will make his key move towards rehabilitating objectivity by stating what is supposed to be obvious. His claim to obviousness should put us on alert. It should because Weber himself has already argued against it – the presumed self-evidence of the facts selected for investigation – and branded the positivist as naive and self-deluding for not recognising that there is nothing self-evident about them. We will adopt the same sceptical attitude here. 'Undoubtedly', Weber says, 'all evaluative ideas are "subjective".... But it *obviously* [my emphasis] does not follow from this that research in the cultural sciences can only have results which are "subjective" in the sense that they are *valid* for one person and not for another. Only the degree to which they interest different persons varies' (1949: 83–84). Research in the cultural sciences may have results that are valid for everyone, despite the fact that all evaluative ideas are subjective – this is what Weber is suggesting. And this should be obvious, he says, even though there is nothing obvious about it. It has been suggested in this respect that Weber had 'a two-tiered approach' to objectivity (e.g. Hoenisch 2006). The first concerns perspective and the selection of facts to be investigated, the second the analysis and interpretation of the facts that have been selected. According to this view, Weber believed that the selection of facts was inherently subjective, but he also believed that once this stage had been passed the social scientist was capable of producing objective results. Not everyone would agree with this interpretation – and with good reason. If this was Weber's last word on the matter he would be accused of the same kind of naiveté and self-deception of which he accused the positivist. If the selection of facts for scientific investigation is subjective, what is there to prevent the selection of certain results over other results for endorsement as valid knowledge from being likewise subjective? Is not analysis and interpretation themselves guided by perspective? It is more likely that this was not Weber's last word on the matter – more likely that he did not have one. For there is no last word. Weber was dealing with an intractable contradiction, and he could not but contradict himself whichever way he chose to go.

Let us return to the quotation above for a closer reading. The results of an investigation, Weber says, are valid not just for the investigator but for other persons as well. In this sense they are not subjective. What may be different, he goes on to say, is not the validity of the results as such but the degree to which these results interest other persons. What is one to make of this statement? If the object selected for investigation is by Weber's own admission not valid for everyone, if it is not objective but subjective – for it does not interest everyone, only the investigator – why should the results of the investigation be treated otherwise? Is this not a contradiction? And is not a contradiction also to say that something is valid but of no interest? As the term itself suggests both in English and German, to be valid something must have value. If it does not interest other persons, it is because it is not relevant and meaningful to them, because it has no value as far as they are concerned. Yet if it has no value, it cannot be valid for them. It is valid only for those persons who take an interest in it. Weber comes close to admitting this in the last sentence of the paragraph: 'Scientific truth is precisely what is *valid* for all who *seek* the truth' (1949: 84).

It may be argued, of course, that something could be valid objectively, irrespective of whether one takes an interest in it or not so that those who ignore it do so to their detriment. Yet to make such an argument one would need to posit a transcendental subject that validates this something and holds it in this state of validation until lesser subjects take an interest in it and come to see it in the same way. This argument is not to be criticised per se. The problem rather – the problem for Weber, that is – is that he cannot make such an argument. It would contradict his own transcendental assumptions, namely, the idea that in and of itself the world is meaningless and that it is human beings who invest it with significance and value:

> The transcendental presupposition of every *cultural science* lies not in our finding a certain culture or any 'culture' in general to be *valuable* but rather in the fact that we are *cultural beings*, endowed with the capacity and the will to take a deliberate attitude towards the world and to *lend it* [my emphases] *significance* (1949: 81).

This is what we do as cultural beings: give the world significance with one hand and take it back with the other. This is what must be done as a matter of course because as Weber himself often pointed out, the world we live in has no significance in and of itself. It has been disenchanted.

We have, then, reached the point from where it becomes apparent that there can be no objectivity in *any* cultural science. Either the results of analysis are selected as valid on the basis of evaluative ideas and are therefore as subjective as the facts selected for analysis, or, alternatively, they are objectively valid, irrespective of whether they are selected or not, because they are validated by a transcendental subject. In the latter case, however, the role of the subject who is supposed to think for itself and produce by itself objective results is rendered superfluous. And so is the whole discussion concerning objectivity. Any way one looks it, objectivity is 'not to be had'.

There is another level of conceptualisation and analysis where objectivity emerges as an impossible condition, and we will turn to it next. This is the hypothetical scenario where the subject (whether individual or collective) somehow manages to purge itself from everything that it has ever taken for granted – by means of a monumental process of exhaustive socioanalysis, let us say. As we shall see shortly, the problem with this hypothetical scenario is that an analysis of this sort would destroy the subject because what it has taken for granted is what makes it what it is. It would destroy the subject as it currently is, but taken to its logical conclusion whereby the entire world becomes transparent, it would destroy the subject as subject. If it could become objective the subject would no longer be subject but object, a being that would know everything but would have no will to do anything. Cultural science is aware of this, at some level anyway, and would probably assert it if the need arises. It would assert it as *cultural* science because it is concerned with meaningful action. But it would also have to deny it as cultural *science*. If it is to be science and not simply another point of view, it must maintain its objectivist pretensions. A classic example of this contradictory attitude, of asserting both the cultural and the scientific at the same time, is the work of Karl Mannheim. Mannheim was one of those thinkers who seem to have truly agonised over the prospect of living with the historical unconscious exposed, hence in a meaningless world. But he was also a thinker who sought to turn the agony into a virtue by portraying it as self-mastery, hence liberation.

Mannheim was probably one of the first in the social sciences to spell out the consequences of using what we would call today social constructionism to expose other points of view as illusions. If the dominant point of view can be exposed as an ideology that strives to maintain the status quo, the dominated point of view that strives to transform the world can equally be exposed as utopia. Such is the main problematic of Mannheim's book; and it remains as much of a problem today as it was at the time he elaborated it. The unintended consequence of this sort of reciprocal unmasking, Mannheim says, was the destruction of 'man's confidence in human thought in general' (1936: 41). Human thought could no longer be relied upon to provide answers to pressing questions about life, and because there was no longer any other kind of thought available – innate ideas and principles having been banished since the seventeenth century – 'man' was left hovering over the void. 'The roots through which human thought had hitherto derived its nourishment were exposed', Mannheim (1936: 42) goes on to say. Is human thought, then, destined to dry up and die like a tree that has been uprooted and is no longer nourished? Such is the agonising question that Mannheim raises: 'How is it possible for man to continue to think and live in a time when the problems of ideology and utopia are being radically raised and thought through in all their implications?' (1936: 42). How, indeed? Having reached this critical point however, Mannheim will retrace his steps. There is salvation around the corner, he says, both for 'man' in general and the epistemic 'man' in particular:

> This is the point where the political problem-complex of ideology and utopia becomes the concern of the sociology of knowledge, and where the scepticism and relativism arising out of the mutual destruction and devaluation of divergent political aims become a means of *salvation*. For this scepticism and relativism compel self-criticism and *self-control* and lead to a new conception of objectivity. What seems to be so unbearable in life itself, namely, to continue to live with the unconscious uncovered, is the historical prerequisite of scientific critical self-awareness. Even in our personal life we become *masters of ourselves* when the unconscious motivations which formerly existed behind our backs suddenly come into our field of vision and thereby become accessible to conscious control (1936: 47; my emphases).

There is much to be said about this quotation, but I shall confine myself to the key issue that concerns us here – the question of attaining objectivity. We have already noted that even if such attainment were possible – which it is not – it would not be an attainment at all, or, at any rate, it would be an attainment that would put an end to all desire for any further attainment. It should be clear that in this extract Mannheim does not see or pretends not to see a problem with objectivity. For him and for the epistemic subject in general the 'unbearable', namely, living with the historical unconscious uncovered, becomes not only bearable but the very means of salvation. The subject is saved from itself, says Mannheim, by becoming master of itself. It may no longer be subject but it is at least autonomous. Later on in the book Manheim will recall a 'prophesy' that highlights what it could mean in practical terms to be objective and autonomous. 'Gottfried Keller's prophesy', he says, namely, that '"the ultimate triumph of freedom will be barren"—begins to assume, for us at least, an ominous meaning' (1936: 250). At this point in the argumentation, however, this prophesy – the paradox of being free to do everything but with no will to do anything – is cast aside.

Mannheim will revisit the issue at the end of his discussion on the utopian mentality, even if what he has to say about it will be cast as something of a warning and does not seem to represent a true change of heart. Even at this stage of the argument, he will insist that the individual is capable of making decisions that *'really'* lie with him' and are truly his decisions and that this feat can be achieved 'by unveiling the hidden motives behind the individual's decisions, thus putting him in a position really to choose' (1939: 262). Yet Mannheim does not completely forget his earlier argument either – the argument, that is, that 'strictly speaking' the subject does not think for itself, but on the basis of what is given to it by society, what he takes for granted. Hence, he is deeply worried about the process of unveiling the historical unconscious. Taken to its logical conclusion, he says, it would lead to the 'complete elimination of reality-transcending elements from our world'. And that, in turn, would generate 'a "matter-of-factness" which ultimately would mean the decay of the human will'. The problem, Mannheim goes on to say, is not so much the elimination of ideology – one of the two reality transcending elements of 'our' world – because this would constitute a crisis for only certain social groups, those in power. The real problem, rather, has to do with the complete elimination of utopias. If that were to happen, the subject would find itself face to face with the 'greatest of all paradoxes' – complete freedom to do everything coupled with a passivity that cares about nothing. Gottfried Keller's 'prophesy' would finally come true. It is worth quoting Mannheim at some length here:

> The disappearance of utopia brings about a static state of affairs in which man himself becomes no more than a *thing*. We would be faced with *the greatest paradox imaginable,* namely, that man, who has achieved the highest degree of rational mas-

tery of existence, left without ideals, becomes a mere creature of impulses. Thus, after a long tortuous, but heroic development, just at the highest stage of awareness, when history is ceasing to be *blind fate*, and is becoming more and more man's own creation, with the relinquishment of utopias, man would lose his will to shape history and therewith his ability to understand it (Mannheim 1936: 262–263; my emphases).

Without utopias, then, without any myths to live by, 'man's' development would be no development at all. It would be a circular journey that would take him back to the point of departure, perhaps even before the point of departure, as Marx will say about a certain revolution (a re-volution, as we shall see in the next chapter). Without any utopias, 'man' would come full circle: from being a thing – mechanically acting out unconscious motivations – to being a thing – lacking the will to do anything. His 'rational mastery of existence' would be completely irrational, based on impulses rather than reason; his 'highest stage of awareness' would also be the lowest because he would no longer have the ability to understand history; and history itself would be what it has always been – the outcome of blind fate.

What is to be done then, to avoid such a monumental crisis? There is nothing that can be done. The crisis of objectivity has always already been a permanent feature of 'our' world. If the subject were to become objective, it would no longer be subject. It would be a subject-less subject, an object, a thing. If it does not become objective, it remains what it has always been – a subject, hence subjective. Any way one looks at it, there can be no such thing as an objective subject. The notion is a contradiction in terms. Any way one looks at it, objectivity is a phantom.

We shall bring the discussion forward in time and towards its end by exploring one last example of recognition of the impossibility of objectivity and its denial at the same time. I have chosen the case of a social theorist who has done more than any other perhaps to further the cause of social constructionism. And I have chosen it precisely because I wish to draw attention to the fact that even in such cases the hope of finding an exit to the circle of the social is not extinguished. 'The sociologist', says Bourdieu in his *Pascalian Meditations*, '*might seem* to be threatened with a kind of schizophrenia, in as much as he is condemned to speak of historicity and relativity in a discourse that aspires to universality and objectivity' (2000: 93; my emphases). The sociologist is not condemned to doing anything, of course. Insofar as he historicizes and relativizes other discourses, this is his choice. He chooses to make history the limit of thought and demonstrate that discourses are relative to the subject that produces them. And he chooses to do so precisely because he can use relativism as a weapon against the subjection of the subject. Bourdieu could not have been clearer on this issue. 'Historicization', he says (2000: 93), 'has been one of the most effective weapons in all the battles of the *Aufklärung* against obscurantism and absolutism and, more generally, against all forms of absolutization or naturalization of the historical and therefore contingent and arbitrary'. And so it has. Yet if everything is 'historical and therefore contingent and arbitrary', if there is nothing absolute, natural, and necessary, how can one claim that one's discourse is universal and objective – a pure gift of thought? One would apparently be denying the possibility and asserting it at the same time. Hence the threat of schizophrenia to which Bourdieu refers or, to be more precise, what 'might seem' as a threat. For what he is suggesting with this turn of phrase is that this is only an apparent threat, not real. But is it only apparent? Can Bourdieu or anyone else for that matter who wishes to save objectivity, avoid contradiction and eliminate the threat of schizophrenia? Let us follow his argumentation closely:

> We have to acknowledge that reason did not fall from heaven as a mysterious and forever inexplicable gift, and that it is therefore historical *through and through;* but we are not forced to conclude, as is often supposed, that it is reducible to history. It is in history, and in history alone, that we must seek the principle of the *relative independence* of reason from the history of which it is the product (2000: 109; my emphases).

I have highlighted the expression 'relative independence' not only as a way of substantiating my earlier claim that this theme of the more or less appears without fail in the writings of all those who assert and at the same time deny the existence of the circle. I have done so also because it will reappear in precisely this form – relative autonomy – in the last chapter, in which I will discuss it in detail. But to return to the substance of the quotation above: it has to be acknowledged that reason is neither a gift from God nor a gift of nature. That much, we should add, has been decided long ago and today the modernist subject cannot bring itself to believe otherwise. What it believes today is that reason is a gift of history and society, historical and social completely and utterly – 'through and through'. This having been said, however, readers are also told that they and the author are not forced to conclude what has just been concluded, namely, that reason is historical through and through. It would seem that they have an option – the option to contradict themselves by saying that it is not reducible to history. For if history is not the sole source of reason by all good logic what is left of it, that which cannot be reduced to history, must be a gift from God or nature – a claim that has just been rejected. The contradiction or the rotation around the circle repeats itself in the last sentence. Although not reducible to history, reason is nonetheless historical through and through. For it is in history – 'and in history alone' – that we must search for what will make reason independent. There are, then, two reasons that make reason historical through and through: it is not a gift from God or nature, and it depends on the historical to make it independent. At this point the rotation around the circle accelerates to a dizzying speed. For what history will make reason independent of is nothing other than itself. Reason depends on history for its independence from history – this is Bourdieu's claim. This is to say, among other things, that *without* history to help it liberate itself reason would be hopelessly *historical*. It is to say this and to take another step closer to the point where schizophrenia breaks in. Yet Bourdieu will not allow this to happen. He will stop pretending that there is no contradiction involved and will admit the reality of the circle. Does not the scientific subject, asks Bourdieu, 'in *some sense* [my emphasis] situate himself outside of the game, which he perceives as such, from an external, superior position, thereby asserting the possibility of a sovereign, totalizing, objective point of view, that of the neutral, impartial spectator?' Indeed, this is precisely what the scientific subject does in 'some sense' – in the sense that situating itself outside the game is nothing more than a figment of its imagination. Bourdieu goes on to admit the inadmissible: 'It cannot be denied', he says, 'that reflexive historico-sociological analysis tends to produce and impose, in a quite *circular* [my emphasis] way, its own criteria of scientificity'. It cannot be denied, but it has to be denied for the sake of the subject who strives desperately to escape the circle that encircles it. 'But is it possible—without invoking a *deus ex machina*—to escape from a *circle* [my emphasis] that is present in reality, and not just in the analysis?' (2000: 117).

It is, of course, not possible. As Bourdieu makes clear the circle is a real, not a figment of the scholastic imagination. It is the very personification of reality – the reality of human finitude. It is even more real, certainly more painful in the reality that the modernist subject has constructed for itself. For this subject cannot invoke a deus ex machina or a *deus* of any sort for that matter. It would go against everything that makes it what it *imagines* itself to be – a subject that thinks for itself and is therefore the master of its own destiny. Hence this subject is destined to remain encircled and to go round and round in circles, all the while deceiving itself and all those who wish to be deceived that it can find an exist and step outside. It is destined to remain subject hence subjective. Subjectivism is the price it has to pay for thinking – a cost of living as real as any monetary cost.

Notes

1. In 'A Letter from a Gentleman to His Friend in Edinburgh', Hume (1993 [1745]: 115–116) tells us that he was charged with, among other things, 'Universal Scepticism ... where he doubts of every Thing... and maintains the Folly of pretending to believe any Thing with Certainty.... Principles leading to down right Atheism by denying the doctrine of Causes and Effects.... Sapping the foundations of Morality, by denying the natural and essential Difference betwixt Right and Wrong, Good and Evil, Justice and Injustice; making the Difference only artificial, and to arise from human Conventions and Compacts'.

2. Although Locke claims that this was the date of the meeting, it must have been earlier because there are drafts of the *Essay* that date from 1671. See note 2 in Locke (1997 [1706]: 750).

3. See Yolton's discussion in *Locke and the Way of Ideas* (1993).

4. Quoted in Yolton (1993: 9).

5. Elsewhere (Argyrou 2003) I have argued that this theory cannot be taken seriously even as a myth.

6. See 'Letter to Christian Jacob Kraus (18 December 1784)', Hamann (1996a [1784]).

CHAPTER 4

POLITICAL ECONOMY

Re-volution

Revolutions revolve. They go round and come round, follow a circular trajectory that takes them back to the point of departure. They were meant to revolve, even if this is not how the term is understood today. It is what it means literally and how it was still understood in the seventeenth century – as a social movement whose aim was to restore an earlier state of affairs. We have Arendt's authority to vouch for this. 'The word [revolution] was first used not when what we call revolution broke out in England and Cromwell rose to the first revolutionary dictatorship'. On the contrary, says Arendt (2006 [1963]: 33), it was first used 'in 1660, after the overthrow of the Rump Parliament and at the occasion of the restoration of the monarchy'. The Glorious Revolution, she goes on to say, 'was not thought of as a revolution at all, but as a restoration of monarchical power to its former righteousness and glory'.

Although revolutions are today understood as progressive movements, this is nothing more than a modernist prejudice. Their aim remains fundamentally what it has always been: re-volution, restoration of an earlier state of affairs, return to the origin, the mythical time at the beginning of time, as we shall see shortly. This desire to return to the beginning is still visible in the case of the American and French Revolutions. As Arendt (2006: 34) notes, 'both were played in their initial stages by men who were firmly convinced that they would do no more than restore an old order of things that had been disturbed and violated by the despotism of absolute monarchy or the abuses of colonial government. They pleaded in all sincerity that they wanted to revolve back to old times when things had been as they ought to be'. Even as the term began to acquire its contemporary meaning, says Arendt (2006: 35), 'Thomas Paine could still, true to the spirit of a bygone age, propose in all earnestness to call the American and French Revolutions by the name of "counter-revolutions"'. This may sound strange coming from a revolutionary, but 'it shows in a nutshell how dear the idea of revolving back, of restoration, was to the hearts and minds of the revolutionaries'. The desire to go back to where things had been as they ought to be is not visible today, certainly not to revolutionaries, but this is only because they are blinded by the rhetoric of progress, the idea that 'man' can make history and become the master of his own destiny, and no doubt the rhetoric of secularism. As Eliade (1959) notes in *The Myth of Eternal Return*, although modern 'man' valorises history (hence also himself) at the expense of myth and the time of the first ancestors and gods, he cannot do without the mythical time of the origin. He too longs for the beginning of time when the world had just been born and was still fresh and pure and copes with the meaningless in life – injustice and suffering – by attaching metaphysical significance to history. In the end and at the end there is salvation. Eliade mentions communism as a paradigmatic example of this desire, but much the same can be said about any modernist revolution, proletarian and bourgeois. The aim of revolution, says Arendt (2006: 1), 'was, and always has been, freedom'. No doubt. It has to be freedom because 'man' was born free and freedom belongs to him by right – a natural, God-given right given at the beginning of time. If he is now everywhere in chains it is because he has fallen into history. He must therefore put an end to it and, as he cannot go back in time, he will end it by pressing forward until he arrives at the end of history, hence also at the beginning of time. Though Arendt thinks it ought not to be, it is well known that the aim of revolution is also equality and fraternity – the brotherhood of 'man'. This too is understandable. In another, related image this is how the world was at the beginning – a world of Edenic bliss, of human unity, purity and innocence.

Such is the modernist imagination. It strives to find salvation in this world. And this is why revolutions revolve or, at least, one of the reasons. They are condemned to re-volution because there is neither an end to history nor a beginning – no time outside time. *In time* and in the *meantime*, revolutions will go round and come round or, to use another geometrical figure, they will go back to square one, replacing one kind of unjust and oppressive society with another – a society, let us say for the sake of argument and to use a recent and fashionable image, that targets the body with a society that targets the soul. If empirical evidence is needed, the historical record is full of re-volutions.

If the aim of revolution is freedom, as Arendt says, there is another aspect to its circularity. This aspect is less visible no doubt because it happens almost instantly or happens always already. Revolutions revolve long before they revolve. From the moment revolutionaries take the given for granted as a grant or gift, they become re-volutionaries. They always already take the given for granted, by definition – not only because they have no other option but to take, but also because if they did not, they would have no reason to revolt. And because they do take the given, they always already give in and give up. This is to say, as we will show later in more detail, that the condition of possibility of freedom is also the condition of its impossibility, namely, conformity. It is this aspect of re-volution with which we will concern ourselves here. We shall examine it as a problem that emerges in the gap between what revolution literally means and the meaning that was subsequently attached to it. And we will look at a proposed solution to this problem. That revolutions revolve is readily recognised in the discourse we will examine. The problem is that they are no longer meant to revolve. Their aim now is to go forward, not backwards, to create something new – a '*novus ordo saeclorum*', as Arendt (2006: 171) says about the American Revolution – not to repeat the old state of affairs. Yet they do repeat, and do so every time. It is as if the term stubbornly refuses to adjust itself to the new meaning, as if revolution is destined to do what was originally assigned to do irrespective of the wishes of subsequent generations of revolutionaries. Indeed, not only do revolutions always revolve, but sometimes they even go back behind their point of departure to a time before their time. They restore forms of state and government far worse than those that the revolution was meant to destroy, as if their trajectory was that of a regressive spiral rather than a circle. This is not our proposition, nor is it our grievance. It is Marx who speaks – the personification of the revolutionary if ever there was one – and we cannot but take what he has to say seriously and attend to it with the thoughtfulness it deserves.

It is in *The Eighteenth Brumaire of Louis Bonaparte* that Marx purports to explain why revolutions revolve, why they turn out to be re-volutions rather than revolutions – on the very first page, in the second paragraph. Let us note, to begin with, that although the book is about a specific revolution, the French Revolution of 1848, what Marx has to say in these first few pages concerns revolution in general. Marx will provide several historical examples to this effect, but he will also, at this early stage, mark an exit to the circle. He will argue that re-volution can be avoided, the circle broken, the revolution put on the right track, which is nothing other than the straight line. He will claim that it is a matter of time (if there is any) before this can be achieved and of practice, a matter of forgetting the past in revolutionary praxis and letting the conditions themselves do all the talking. At a certain irreversible point in this process, Marx will argue, the revolutionaries will jump and the future will appear and become (a) present.

> Men make their own history, but they do not make it just as they *please*; they do not make it under circumstance chosen by themselves, but under circumstances directly encountered, *given* and transmitted from the past. The tradition of all the dead generations weighs like a nightmare on the brain of the living (Marx 1963 [1852]: 15; my emphases).

These are famous words. They have been quoted innumerable times, have inspired innumerable people, and we cannot help approaching them with a certain degree of trepidation, especially because our aim is to analyse them critically. All the more reason therefore to read them as closely and carefully as possible. We shall interpret the opening line as an attempt to set the record straight by turning Hegel upside down or on his head, as it is sometimes said in the Marxist tradition. For Marx it is 'men' who make history, not some mysterious force working behind their back and beyond their control – the Hegelian Spirit. Nonetheless, there is a *but* – for things are not as simple they appear. Having put 'men' resolutely in charge of history, Marx will go on immediately, in the same sentence and in one breath, to qualify the assertion. 'Men' make history but not just as they like, not under circumstances that they themselves have chosen. The circumstances have been *given* to them by the dead generations – as a gift, no doubt – even though Marx is certain that it is nothing other than an unbearable burden, a horrible nightmare. The circumstances have been given and the 'men' who will make their own history have taken them. They have been receptive to them – but what would they have to give in return or, rather, what have they already given?

There is a pleonasm in Marx's statement, but he will be unable to do without it. It goes or should go without saying that 'men' will make history (if this is what they do) under circumstances they have not chosen. If they could choose the circumstances under which they lived, life would be 'pleasing' to them, and if it was pleasing, they would have no reason to change it, no need to make (any more) history. The circumstances chosen would be history having already been made (a) present – an auto-gift. To make history 'men' must live under circumstances they have not chosen and which are not to their liking. This is an irreducible condition. It is the very condition of possibility of making history. But it is also, at the same time, the very condition of impossibility of making history, if by this we understand what 'making history' is meant to mean – becoming master of one's destiny. If 'men' have no option but to make history under circumstances they have not chosen, they will never make history or, at any rate, not their *own* history. The best they will ever be able to do is to make the history that history itself makes possible for them to make – possible, understood in this context as thinkable, imaginable and desirable. This is what they give back to the dead generations for having taken from them. It is how they give in and give up the prospect of becoming masters of their own destiny. The real masters are the dead who direct them from their graves.

Because this claim could be read as another sociological argument of reproduction of the type structure-agency-structure, a few qualifications may be in order before proceeding further. To say that revolutions revolve is not to deny the possibility of social transformation. There is no doubt that they do transform, but this is already to say that what they change is the *form* of the social order not the *content*. If the aim of revolution has always been freedom, there is no revolution that has ever achieved this goal, not even the proletarian revolutions that Marx envisaged. If anything, they turned out to be worse than the bourgeois revolutions of the eighteenth century and proved Marx right in one thing: revolutions not only revolve but often go back behind their point of departure, establishing regimes far more oppressive than the regimes they were meant to replace. There is, then, what appears in the aftermath of revolutions – the form, which is transformed – and what does not appear – the *desired* content, freedom – or, what is another way of saying the same thing, the *phenomenon* of change and change itself. The gap between the two is the irreducible gap we have encountered in various guises – commodity and gift, the meantime and time itself, beings and Being, the phenomenon and the phantom, or thing in itself. It is the gap that is more often than not ignored – an ignorance that allows the subject to present the phantom as a real, living being. Let us also note here in passing that if there is (still) a debate in the social sciences about structure and agency, this too is the result of ignoring this gap and conflating the phenomenon of change with change itself. As the etymology of the term itself suggests, change is exchange, substituting one thing for another – in this case one type of social hierarchy with a different type.

We have been saying that Marx will be unable to do without the pleonasm we have noted. He must say what is not necessary to say not only because he wants to explain why revolutions revolve and fail to fulfil their promise, not only because he wants to bring to our attention the nightmare that burdens the living, but also because he wants the revolutionaries to wake up from this terrible dream. He must say it, in short, because he is convinced there is a solution to the problem of re-volution:

> And just when they [men] seem engaged in revolutionizing themselves and things, in creating something that has never yet existed, precisely in such periods of revolutionary crisis, they anxiously conjure up the spirits of the past to their service and *borrow* from them names, battle cries and costumes in order to present the new scene of world history in this time-honoured disguise and this *borrowed* language. Luther donned the mask of the Apostle Paul, the Revolution of 1789 to 1814 draped itself alternatively as the Roman republic and the roman empire, and the Revolution of 1848 knew nothing better to do than to parody, now 1789, now the revolutionary tradition of 1793 to 1795 (1963 [1852]: 15; my emphases).

The nightmare that weighs on the brain of the living is the borrowing from the dead generations and the cost that this implies – the borrowing of names, battle cries, costumes, masks, a language to speak with about the present and the future. It is because they borrow from the dead and are indebted to them that 'men' fail to create what has never yet existed. The best they can ever do under such circumstances is to recreate what has gone before. Living 'men' take from dead 'men' and because they take, they give in to them. They repeat the past, often at the most critical moment in the struggle, and give up the prospect of becoming masters of their own destiny. Just when they are about to revolutionize themselves and the world, at that very moment, things get out of hand – for no one really had a firm grasp on them to begin with. Things change hands – from the dead to the living and back – the revolution revolves and the world returns to the point of departure. It is even the case that sometimes the nightmare or the debt weigh so heavy on the brains of the revolutionaries that events such as those of 1848 are not worthy of the name revolution. They are a parody of earlier revolutions and a farce.

What Marx sketches here, without necessarily being aware that this is what he is doing, is the outline of an economy. We shall call it, not unreasonably, a political economy. It is political because it is about power and 'men's' struggles to liberate themselves. And it is an economy in the twofold sense we have highlighted in the previous chapter. It is an economy firstly, in the sense of limitation – the limitation to what can be done to liberate oneself from the powers that be, an action-(and production) possibility boundary beyond which no one seems able to venture. It is an economy also in the sense of exchange or circle – the circle in which what the revolutionary subject does to liberate itself comes back to confirm its dependence on the powers that be. The question here, as elsewhere, is whether this economy can be overcome, whether the revolutionary subject can find within itself what it needs to make history so that it no longer borrows from the dead, in short, whether it can step outside the circle. We have argued in the last chapter, following Marx himself or, at any rate, one of his 'spectres', as Derrida (2006) says, that there can be no auto-gifts of thought. No one can think for oneself if by thinking for oneself we mean what the claim was meant to mean – thinking *ex nihilo*. Everyone inevitably takes and lives on *borrowed* time hence everyone gives (to others as much as to oneself) what one does not have, that is, nothing. Let us note here that the spectre of Marx we have just referred to is the spectre that appears in the *German Ideology*. There Marx argued that it is not 'man's' consciousness that determines his life but life that determines his consciousness. There as here, it is a matter of borrowing, being indebted to life and to the dead generations. In the present text however, Marx or one of his spectres will forget this debt. And he will ask us to forget it ourselves, to suspend the maxim of the *German Ideology*, even if only once, so that the proletarian revolution can proceed and consummate itself.

Marx then highlights the limits to what 'men' can do with respect to making history and liberating themselves, but he is certainly not about to put Hegel back on his feet. He highlights these limits with the view of demonstrating their own limitations, the way they can be overcome. For unlike the Hegelian spirit, society and history have been made by 'men' and Marx reckons that if it is 'men' who have made them, dead though they now are, it is only reasonable to assume that they can remake them. If society and history have been constructed, they could be deconstructed and perhaps also reconstructed so that something that has never yet existed can be brought into being. How then, does Marx propose to exorcise the ghosts of the past and put them to rest, pay the debt owed to the dead and be done with them? We shall follow him closely in his laborious manoeuvring to escape the circle of political economy. And we will begin where he begins – with an analogy. Revolution, Marx will suggest, is like learning a new language. The subject falters at the beginning but eventually succeeds in mastering the new language and speaks it without having to rely on the old:

> In a like manner a beginner who has learnt a new language always translates it back into his mother tongue, but he has assimilated the spirit of the new language and can freely express himself in it only when he finds his way in it without recalling the old and forgets his native tongue in the use of the new (1963 [1852]: 15–16).

It is unavoidable that one will use the old to acquire the new, Marx seems to be suggesting here. It could not have been otherwise. The subject has no option but to take – indeed, it has always already taken – but this does not mean that it is forever condemned to remain dependent. It can become so proficient in the new that it no longer needs the old and can afford to forget it. Forgetting the debt is undoubtedly one way of breaking any cycle of reciprocity. The living would then be delivered from the dead, the present and the future from the weight of the past. Yet as Derrida (2006) notes in his own discussion of Marx's text, this forgetting is not as simple as it might appear. If the subject were to forget the past, it would also forget why it began and would have no reason to continue. It must, therefore, not forget the past if the acquisition of the new language would have any meaning or the revolution any prospects of success. We have encountered this problem already in our discussion of the epistemic subject. Marx is about to encounter it is his own discussion of the political subject – the revolutionary. In the discussion of the epistemic subject we noted, following Mannheim's own laborious manoeuvring, that the subject that manages to strip itself from everything that it has taken for granted in its attempt to become objective will become a subject-less subject, a subject with no desire to do anything – a thing. It must, therefore, not discard everything. It must retain some sort of historical unconscious, something that it takes for granted, a utopia of one sort or another that will provide direction and meaning in its life. As we shall see, Marx is well aware of this. He will call this absolutely essential element the spirit of the revolution and will contrast it with its spectre or ghost – the dead letter that repeats the same. The subject must not forget the past because part of it, the most important part at that, is the spirit of the revolution. Yet if it does not forget, it will remain a beginner, always translating the new language back into the old unable to master it, always using the old revolutions as a model for the new, hence never becoming quite able to escape the past and create a free society. Forgetting produces the same, remembering retains the same. It seems that whatever the subject does, it is always at the beginning, either because it has never really begun (creating a new society) or because it has come back to the beginning (the revolution produces nothing new or, at least, not the new that is desired – freedom). But perhaps a compromise can be reached. The subject could select to remember what it needs and forget what is not necessary:

> Consideration of this conjuring up of the dead of world history reveals at once a *salient difference* [my emphasis].... The heroes as well as the parties and the masses of the old French Revolution performed *the task of their time* [my emphasis] in Roman costume and with Roman phrases, the task of unchaining and setting up modern *bourgeois* society.... The new social formation once established, the antediluvian Colossi disappeared and with them resurrected Romanity.... Wholly absorbed in the production of wealth and in peaceful competitive struggle, [the bourgeoisie] no longer comprehended that ghosts from the days of Rome watched over its cradle.... They found ... the self-deceptions that they needed in order to conceal from themselves the bourgeois limitations of the content of their struggles and to keep their enthusiasm on the high plane of the historical strategy. Similarly ... Cromwell and the English people had borrowed speech, passions and illusions from the Old Testament for their bourgeois revolution. When the real aim had been achieved, when the bourgeois transformation of English society had been accomplished, Locke supplanted Habakkuk (1963 [1852]: 16–17).

The old French Revolution appeared on the scene of world history with a borrowed costume and spoke with a borrowed language, the costume and language of Rome. And so did the English bourgeois revolution a century earlier. The Old Testament provided the language to speak with passion about the English revolution and what it was meant to achieve. This was perhaps unavoidable. To give oneself a new society one has to take from the old. We should recall that this borrowing is precisely what Marx criticises in the second paragraph of his text. It is why 'men' make history but not quite, why revolution revolves, why the structures of power find ways and means to reinstate themselves. Yet at this point in the discussion Marx will be content to let this borrowing pass by silently or let it off lightly. It is, after all, *bourgeois* revolutions that he is referring to, and as every 'real' revolutionary knows, the content of these struggles is limited. The bourgeoisie knew this too – hence the self-deceptions that they found to conceal from themselves the limitations of their revolution. But Marx has an additional and far more important reason for not making an issue of the borrowings of the bourgeois revolutions. He wishes to commend it, even if not exactly wholeheartedly. He has reached the point where the critique of borrowing from the dead will become something of a praise. He is preparing to compare the bourgeois revolutions with the Revolution of 1848, to highlight the 'salient difference' between them that we have highlighted in the passage above. And he will argue that despite their limitations bourgeois revolutions borrowed something essential from the past that the Revolution of 1848 completely lacked. This something is nothing other than the spirit of the revolution. It is true that once the bourgeois revolutions accomplished their aim, this spirit was completely forgotten. The French no longer comprehended that ghosts from Rome 'watched over the cradle' of their revolution. And the English were quick to replace a prophet of the Old Testament with a bourgeois philosopher. But before amnesia set in, these revolutions at least 'performed the task of their time'. The Revolution of 1848 by contrast accomplished nothing. It was nothing more than a farce and parody:

> Thus the awakening of the dead in those revolutions served the purpose of glorifying the new struggles, not of *parodying* the old; of magnifying the given task in imagination, not of fleeing from its solution in reality; of finding once more the *spirit of revolution,* not of making its *ghost* walk about again. From 1848 to 1851 only the ghost of the old revolution walked about... (1963 [1852]: 17; my emphases).

This is the point, Derrida (2006:140) notes in his own discussion of The Eighteenth Brumaire, 'that Marx intends to distinguish between the spirit (*Geist*) of the revolution and its specter (*Gespenst*)' – or ghost in the translation above. As we have already noted, Marx needs this distinction because this is also the point in the discussion where the critique of borrowing from the dead will turn into praise. It is the point where Marx will argue that what ought to be forgotten – the past – should not be forgotten after all, that it should be forgotten and not forgotten. It is the point, in short, where he comes face to face with the intractable contradiction he is dealing with – that the past is both the condition of possibility of the revolution and the condition of its impossibility, both spirit and spectre, gift and poison – and he will attempt to find ways and means of escaping it. The bourgeois revolutions awoke the dead and borrowed from them, but this was a good kind of borrowing or, at any rate, good enough. It served the purpose of exalting these struggles, of highlighting the true scale of the task ahead, of finding the spirit that is necessary for any revolution to go forward and consummate itself. The Revolution of 1848 by contrast, turned away from the task before it and could only parody the old revolutions. What it retrieved from the past was not the spirit that animates life and makes history but the dead letter, the ghost that make revolutions revolve and go back to the point of departure – indeed, as Marx will note, in this particular case behind the point of departure: 'Instead of *society* having conquered a new content for itself, it seems that the *state* only returned to its oldest from ... Society now seems to have fallen back behind its point of departure' (1963 [1852]: 18–19).

Although Marx distinguishes between the spirit of the revolution and its ghost and although, as Derrida (2006:138) says, he 'holds to this difference as he holds to life', he is 'perhaps as aware as we are of the essential contamination of spirit (*Geist*) by specter (*Gespenst*)' (2006:141). Whatever the case, he will change tactics. Marx 'detests all ghosts, the good and the bad', Derrida goes on to say, and wants to be done with them, put them to rest once and for all. 'It is as if he were saying to us, we who do not believe a word of it: ... anachrony is precisely anachronistic. That fate weighed on the revolutions of the past. Those that are coming ... must turn away from the past, from its *Geist* as well as its *Gespent*.

In sum, they must cease to inherit' (Derrida 2006: 141–142). At some point in his text then, Marx will decide to do away with the dead. Unlike the historical materialism of Benjamin (1968: 257), which posits an 'angel of history' who will 'awaken the dead and make whole what has been smashed', Marx wants the dead to bury themselves by themselves and leave the living alone. Yet the problem remains. If the revolutions that are coming turn away from the past and cease to inherit, if they no longer borrow from the dead, where will they find what they need to come? To whom or to what should they turn? They should turn to their own content, Marx says, which they will discover in reality, though revolutionary praxis itself:

> The social revolution of the nineteenth century cannot draw its poetry from the past, but only from *the future*. It cannot begin with itself before it has stripped off all superstition in regard to the past. Earlier revolutions required recollections of past world history in order to drug themselves concerning their own content. In order to arrive at its own content, the revolution of the nineteenth century must let the dead bury their dead. There the *phrase* went beyond the content; here the content goes beyond the phrase (Marx 1963 [1852]: 18; my emphases).

I have highlighted the word *phrase* because it seems an odd term to use in conjunction with the word *content*. One would have thought that *form* would be more appropriate in this context. The choice of *phrase* seems odd until one recalls that it also appears in the *German Ideology* – and for a very specific reason. There, Marx is arguing against the Young Hegelians who conceived of the struggle to liberate 'man' as a struggle against the products of consciousness, 'conceptions, thoughts, ideas ... to which they attribute an independent existence'. For the Young Hegelians the task was to change human consciousness, which, Marx says, 'amounts to a demand to interpret reality in another way, i.e. to recognise it by means of another interpretation'. Some of them, he goes on to say, 'have found the correct expression for their activity when they declare they are only fighting against "phrases"' (1974 [1846]: 41). *Phrases*, then, are concepts, thoughts, ideas, representations of reality. The Young Hegelians gave them priority over reality itself, and this is exactly what happened with the bourgeois revolutions, according to Marx. In this case, too, 'the phrase went beyond the content', representation beyond reality. This reversal of priorities was not quite the idealism of the Young Hegelians perhaps or the hubris of thought without limits that we noted in our discussion of Bourdieu. Bourgeois revolutions used recollections from the past for a specific purpose – to hide their content from themselves. They deceived themselves on purpose. The social revolution of the nineteenth century by contrast does not need to drug itself with illusions. It must dispel the superstitions of the past before it even begins, must begin before it begins. It is only in this way that it will arrive at its content and see itself as it truly is. Not that it is a question of matching phrase and content, representation and reality at this stage. Although the social revolution of the nineteenth century will draw its poetry from the future rather than the past, it would be premature and idealistic to do this matching now. The content will have to go beyond the phrase, reality given priority over representation. For the whole point of this exercise, as Marx famously said in the 'Theses on Feuerbach', is not to interpret reality, to represent it in yet another way, but to change it. It is presumably only at the end of the revolution when reality has been completely transformed that representation will have something reliable to say. Born of the new and undistorted reality, it will match it precisely, represent it as it truly is, make it (a) present to itself. Until then, representation is a liability.

We are interpreting here, of course, but we are doing so on the basis of what Marx has been saying in these early pages of *The Eighteenth Brumaire* and by keeping in mind one of his most fundamental concepts – his materialist conception of history. If this interpretation is anything to go by, Marx's argument anticipates by more than a century the solution proposed in identity politics for a structurally similar problem. As we shall see in detail in the last section, in this case, too, identifying the content of the struggle is seen by many as a liability, a taking from the powers that be, which can only mean giving in to them. The temptation to identify the self in this politics must therefore be resisted, the identity subverted and destabilised or at the very least recognised for what it is – changing and provisional, hence nothing to lean on firmly. Identity should hold itself open to the future for as long as possible and avoid speedy determination of its content. Not that identity politics is revolutionary in the sense that Marx understood the term, even if it is certainly re-volutionary. As Wendy Brown notes, these forms of struggle are contextual and historically specific. They emerge as a reaction to specific forms of domination and because of this, they are inevitably limited. Marx's vision, on the other hand, Brown goes on to say, was different. 'True human emancipation, achieved at the end of history, conjured for Marx not simply liberation from particular constrains but freedom that was both thoroughgoing and permanent, freedom that was neither partial nor evasive but temporally and spatially absolute.' However, Brown will go on to say – for there is a *however*, as in all such cases – even Marx was unable to escape context and history, despite his universal vision. 'However, since true human emancipation *eventually* acquired for Marx a negative referent (capitalism) and positive content (abolition of capitalism), in time it too would reveal its profoundly historicized and thus limited character' (Brown 1995: 7–8; my emphasis). Brown presents Marx's failure to escape context and history as something he could have avoided. It was only eventually, she says, that emancipation acquired a negative referent and a positive content – and not always already, as we have been arguing – as if it is possible for a notion to occur to someone without a particular referent and a specific content, an idea that appears from nowhere, a deus ex machina, as Bourdieu says. This is also what Marx expects us to believe in the quotation above. He expect us to believe that the revolutionaries will draw their inspiration from the future, which is to say from nowhere, as it has not happened yet, that they will struggle for no particular reason and with no particular aim in mind until they 'arrive at the content of their struggle', at which time they will know why they have been struggling to begin with.

As we have said, identity politics is not concerned with changing the material conditions of existence. If anything, one could accuse it of what Marx accuses the Young Hegelians in *The German Ideology* – being concerned with thinking the world otherwise, of interpreting it in yet another way. Nonetheless, the question of identification, the refusal to pin down and describe what one is and what one is doing, to fill representation with ontological content prematurely is as much of key strategic aim for identity politics as it was for Marx, in this context at least. Recoiling from identification is precisely what he had in mind for the proletarian revolutions of the nineteenth century:

> Bourgeois revolutions, like those of the eighteenth century, storm swiftly from success to success … but they are short-lived; soon they have attained their zenith, and a long crapulent depression lays hold of society before it learns soberly to *assimilate* the results of its storm-and-stress period. On the other hand, proletarian revolutions, like those of the nineteenth century, criticize themselves constantly, interrupt themselves continually in their own course, come back to the apparently accomplished in order to begin it afresh … seem to throw down their adversary only in order that he may draw new strength from the earth and rise again, more *gigantic*, before them, recoil ever and anon from the *indefinite prodigiousness* of their own aims, until a situation has been created which makes all *turning back* impossible, and the *conditions themselves cry out*: Hic, Rhrodus, hic salta! Here is the rose, here dance [original emphases] (1963 [1852]: 19).

The proletarian revolutions of the nineteenth century will criticise and interrupt themselves constantly. They will persist in turning against themselves because they know that if they do not do so they will not be able to avoid turning back. They know only too well about re-volutions, and they have the bourgeois revolutions of the eighteenth century to thank for this insight; for this is precisely what happened to them. They revolved, rotated, went back to the point of departure, replaced the feudal structures of power with their own. The proletarian revolutions by contrast will do everything it takes to avoid this fate. And what it takes is time, if there is any. They will take their time and arrive at their own content one step at a time. For, although they have an aim, its magnitude is still indefinite. They can sense it perhaps, but do not quite fully grasp it yet. And that is how revolutionary practice ought to be. The proletarian revolutions will recoil repeatedly from the temptation to identify their content, define it, and fix it once and for all. It is not time yet and they know it. They also know that they will know when it is time, when the right time comes, when it has arrived and is (a) present. The 'conditions themselves' will tell them. They will 'cry out' loud and clear for everyone to hear.

Marx has a penchant for the dramatic, no doubt. His description of the proletarian revolutions is the description of an epic battle, a battle of giants, a true *gigantomachia*. At times his discourse verges on the poetic, but there is no doubt that it is also positivist to the core. Marx wants the facts to speak for themselves – the conditions to cry out. Yet having awakened the dead, having summoned the spirit of the revolution and allowed it to circulate freely in his text, he will not be able to exorcise it as easily as one might think. The 'conditions themselves' cannot compete with it no matter how loud they cry. The spectre is there and has been there from the very beginning. It is there and orchestrates everything, from the beginning to the end – which is also the beginning. Understandably, Marx does not want to draw much attention to it. He needs it but he does not want it to occupy centre stage. He would have preferred if it was not on the stage at all, if it was completely behind the scenes, if the conditions themselves did all the talking and acting. But he knows that he cannot exorcise it completely, and he will therefore attempt to marginalise it. It is indistinct and indeterminate, he says, prodigious but indefinite, a passing shadow perhaps that is best left alone. Certainly, Marx does not want anyone to touch it or get close to it. And if 'ever and anon' anyone does, they will recoil from it as one does when one sees a ghost.

Marx is encircled by the circle of political economy, and he is searching for an exit. He knows that borrowing from the dead is like selling one's soul to the devil. They will claim it – always already do – and one would have no option but to give in to this claim. If the proletarian revolutions of the nineteenth century must take, they will have to give (in and up). They should take nothing, therefore, not even the spirit of the revolution. They will begin without a spirit and without an aim, without knowing where they are going or whether they are going or coming. Or if this is impossible, if the spirit is necessary to animate the revolution and the aim necessary for the revolution to take aim at something or someone, then perhaps the phrase may be allowed to have some content after all. As for the rest, it will be given, as a gift no doubt, by the conditions themselves along the way. The battle of giants then – the *gigantomachia* – will be the battle of combatants who do not really know one another and have met accidentally, have little appetite for a fight and only a vague idea as to why and for what they are expected to fight. But once they begin, everything will fall into place. The rose will appear from nowhere – a deus ex machina – and will ask them to jump, in this case, at one another.

The Hegemonic

The problem of stepping outside every context and all history, of avoiding taking anything from the past, not even the spirit of the revolution, hence the problem also of re-volution, has bedevilled Marxism long after Marx. It has bedevilled even the most culturally oriented of Marxist discourses, those that rejected Marx's positivism and did not treat spirits, phrases, ideas as ideologies or superstitions that can be disposed of at will and thrown away in the wastebasket of history. Even among discourses that conceptualise domination as a hegemonic rather than an ideological process, consent as the result of internalisation of the social in practice rather than of manipulation and mystification at the discursive level, it is still assumed that revolutionary activity is possible without prior receptivity. If there is a problem – and according to the text we will examine, there is one, a 'major' problem 'with immediate effect' – it is of a different order. It is a problem of identification, of forging the conceptual tools that would be able to identify revolutionary activity of this sort when it appears. The possibility of a revolution without prior receptivity itself is never seriously questioned. I will consider here a classic statement of this position – classic in its attempt to avoid the more positivist aspects of Marx and subsequent Marxist discourses – Raymond William's discussion of the concept of hegemony as an alternative to ideology.

For Williams the notion of hegemony provides a much more realistic and accurate description of class domination than ideology, but it, too, can lead into problems if it is not handled with care. One possible problem, according to Williams, is the use of hegemony in abstract and totalising terms, in which case it becomes compatible with the equally abstract and totalising notion of superstructure and 'even "ideology"' and loses its analytical edge. Hegemony, Williams argues, is a process not a structure or system and as a process it is never total and absolute. To capture reality as accurately as possible therefore, hegemony must be supplemented with a few additional concepts:

> In practice ... hegemony can never be singular. Its internal structures are highly complex.... Moreover (and this is crucial, reminding us of the necessary thrust of the concept), it does not just passively exist as a form of dominance. It has continually to be renewed, recreated, defended and modified. It is also continually resisted, limited, altered, challenged by pressures *not at all its own*. We have then to add to the concept of hegemony the concepts of *counter-hegemony* and *alternative hegemony*, which are real and persistent elements of practice.... The reality of the cultural process must then always include the efforts and contributions of those *who are in one way or another outside or at the edge of the terms of the specific hegemony* (Williams (1977: 112–113; my emphases).

It is should be clear that the supplementary concepts proposed here are 'counter-hegemony' and 'alternative hegemony'. Williams will subsequently become careless in the use of these concepts – not accidentally, as we shall see, as clarity and consistency will lead his exposition into intractable problems and contradictions. All the more reason therefore to clarify these concepts before proceeding any further. We will do so on the basis of the general drift of Williams's argument.

The more important of the two for the purposes of the present discussion is the concept of 'alternative hegemony'. We will take it to mean, using Williams's own terminology, a pressure on hegemony which is not at all its own, not produced by hegemony in other words, an effort or contribution by those who are outside the hegemony in question – outside, 'in one way or another', says Williams vaguely, when the important issue is to know which way exactly, indeed, whether it is possible at all to step outside. We shall also take *counter-hegemony* to mean what it says, an opposition to hegemony by those who are located at its edge or within it. Having set up the argument in this way, Williams will go on to state the problem that the theoretician of the revolution faces. And he will do so breathlessly:

> The *major* theoretical problem, *with immediate effect* on methods of analysis, is to distinguish between alternative and oppositional initiatives and contributions which are made *within* or against a specific hegemony (which then sets certain *limits* to them or which can succeed in *neutralizing*, changing or actually incorporating them) and *other kinds* of initiatives and contributions which are *irreducible* to the terms of the original or the adaptive hegemony and are in *that sense independent* (1977: 114; my emphases).

Let us note, to begin with, that alternative hegemony has now shifted position. It is no longer outside hegemony but within it, hence no longer alternative. It is now oppositional, or counter-hegemonic. One might think that this is because Williams has changed his mind in the meantime and no longer believes in the possibility of an alternative hegemony, but apparently such is not the case. He will maintain that initiatives and contributions by revolutionary forces outside hegemony are still possible, even though he does not appear to know what they might be. At any rate, he will now refer to them vaguely – 'other kinds' of initiatives and contributions. Be that as it may, because these other kinds of initiatives and contributions come from the outside, they are irreducible to the hegemony in question and independent of it. This is presumably what Williams would have liked to say, but he does not quite say it. There seems to be a slight hesitation in his formulation of these ideas. One presumes that he would have liked these initiatives and contributions to be independent in every sense – absolutely independent – but he will not risk such a totalising statement. He will say rather that they are independent in a specific sense – 'in that sense' – which suggests that in another sense, whatever that might be, they may not be absolutely independent. Why this hesitation? By all good logic, if initiatives and contributions come from the outside, if they are irreducible to hegemony, they ought to be completely independent. Having shed everything that did not properly belong to them, they cannot be reduced any further. They are now 'irreducible', properly themselves, hence, independent of everything else in every sense. Williams is not so certain, however. If anything, he is about to admit that things are not as simple as they might appear. The problem, it turns out, is not simply theoretical or analytical, not just a question of becoming adept in identifying revolutionary initiatives and contributions that are irreducible to hegemony. It is much more serious than that. It seems that even if one had the necessary conceptual tools, one would not be able to identify initiatives and contributions of this sort because they are nowhere to be found:

> It can be persuasively argued that *all* or *nearly all* initiatives and contributions, even when they take on *manifestly* alternative or oppositional forms, are in practice tied to the hegemonic: that the dominant culture, so to say, at *once produces and limits its own forms of counter-culture*. There is more evidence for this view (for example in the case of the Romantic critique of industrial civilization) than we usually admit. But there is evident variation [and] ... it would be wrong to overlook the importance of works and ideas which, while clearly affected by hegemonic limits and pressures, are at least *in part* significant breaks *beyond* them, which may again *in part* be neutralized, reduced, or incorporated, but which in their most active elements nevertheless *come through as* independent and original (1977: 114; my emphases).

Williams manoeuvres laboriously in this quotation. Although all initiatives and contributions are in practice tied to the hegemonic, on second thought, it is not all but 'nearly all'. Some works and ideas are clearly affected by hegemonic limits, but they are also 'significant breaks beyond them' or at least they are beyond them 'in part'. Let us note here before proceeding further what does not fail to appear in all such apologetics, the question, encountered so many times already, of the partially, the relatively and the more or less – which, as we have said, we will examine in the last chapter. The key issue for us in this quotation, at any rate, is Williams's recognition that it is the dominant culture that produces countercultures. They are its own, he says; it creates them and gives them the spirit that animates them. And because it gives them what they need to come to life – the spirit of opposition, if not revolution – it also sets limits to what they can do to evade its grasp. In this text Williams anticipates by more than a decade the same recognition that, as we shall see below, one finds in identity politics, and the question here as there is whether there is anything that can be done to escape the hold that hegemony has over the countercultures that it itself produces. Understandably, Williams wishes to keep the door open or at least slightly ajar to such a possibility. He knows that he is caught in the circle we have called political economy, but he does not wish to admit the finality of the encirclement. Hence, although *all* countercultural initiatives and contributions are at once produced and limited by the dominant culture, on second thought, it is not exactly all. It is nearly all. Some of them, it seems, have managed to escape this predicament. They are neither produced nor limited by the dominant culture. They have been conceived beyond it and operate outside it. Williams will go on to state another contradiction: '[A]uthentic breaks *within* and *beyond* [the cultural process] ... have *often in fact* occurred' (1977: 114; my emphases).

We do not know how often the breaks within and especially beyond have occurred or if they have occurred at all because Williams will not substantiate this 'fact' with any facts. He will simply state it as a fact that stands on its own. It would be difficult to substantiate it anyway. Certainly, the claim that authentic breaks can occur within the dominant culture is untenable. If they occur within, they are not authentic; by definition they are tied to the hegemonic culture and are derivative. By the same token if they are authentic, they cannot be authentic in part and in part neutralised, reduced, or incorporated. They are either authentic or inauthentic. By all good logic, to be both is to be neither. There is of course another possibility, which, as we have said, Kant first introduced in order to resolve 'antinomies' of this sort and which we will revisit in the discussion on identity politics below. Breaks may be authentic, independent, and original in one sense – in the imagination – and inauthentic, dependent, and derivative in another – in reality. As Williams himself says in the quotation above, they come through *as* authentic, independent, and original. They look as if they are, appear to be in this way, but this is only an appearance, the phenomenon of a phantom. In reality they are nothing of the sort. The Kantian distinction is just about the only way to avoid the contradiction of being and not being the same thing at the same time. One creates a mythical reality alongside the empirical world and escapes to it whenever the need arises.

The question of whether there can be any countermovements independent of the dominant culture, hence revolutionary but not re-volutionary, is not only an empirical question. If it were, it would be a matter of identifying such movements in history and demonstrating that they have succeeded in liberating society. As we have already noted, if there is anything that the proletarian revolutions of the twentieth century demonstrated is precisely what Marx complained about with respect to the Revolution of 1848 – that it went back *behind* its point of departure. What we are concerned with here, at any rate, is the theoretical aspect of the question, the question of the source of the spirit of the revolution – the ideas that are necessary to generate any revolution or opposition and the values that make these ideas relevant and meaningful and give them motivational force. I shall examine two well-known treatments of the issue, Bourdieu's discussion of symbolic power and James Scott's study of peasant resistance.

Bourdieu begins his discussion in the traditional sociological manner, with the assumption of unanimity and therefore conformity, what he calls *doxa*, and raises the question of the emergence of discord, which he calls *heterodoxy*. The question, in other words, is how what was previously taken for granted by everyone concerned becomes something to be questioned, criticised and rejected. Barring a deus ex machina, a spirit of some sort that comes from nowhere in an instant and makes people 'jump', Bourdieu argues that the condition of possibility of social critique is 'objective crisis':

> The practical questioning of [doxa] implied in a particular way of living that is brought about by 'cultural contact' or by the political and economic crises correlative with class division is not the purely intellectual operation which phenomenology designates by the term *epoche*, the deliberate, methodical suspension of naive adherence to the world. The critique which brings the undiscussed into discussion, the unformulated into formulation, has as the condition of its possibility *objective crisis*, which in *breaking with the immediate fit between the subjective structures and the objective structures* destroys self-evidence practically (Bourdieu 1977: 168–169).

Bourdieu's point is clear. There needs to be some sort of crisis for the dominated to begin questioning their conditions of existence, a crisis that breaks the correspondence between the subjective and the objective, that is, the expectations that the dominated have and the real possibilities for fulfilling these expectations. Unlike Marx, however, Bourdieu will not argue that facts can speak for themselves. Crisis is necessary but not enough. As he will go on to say, '[C]risis is a necessary condition for the questioning of doxa but is not in itself a sufficient condition for a critical discourse'. What is necessary over and above any crisis is 'the material and symbolic means of rejecting the [dominant] definition of the real' (Bourdieu 1977: 169). We shall not concern ourselves here with the material means. We shall focus instead on what is of direct relevance to the present discussion, the symbolic means – the ideas and values needed to formulate a critical discourse, imagine an alternative reality, and mobilise the dominated into action. Where do they come from? Bourdieu has already indicated one possible source of such ideas and values – 'cultural contact'. They come from the outside, from another society, and they are received, to the extent that they are, because the dominated in question are receptive to them on account of the crisis. To put it schematically, once the gap between objective and subjective structures opens up and questions about society raised, the dominated need answers to them. If ideas and values from another society can provide those answers, they will be adopted and used to formulate a critique.

It could be argued perhaps that because these ideas come from the outside, they are independent of, and irreducible to, the dominant culture in question, and this is no doubt true. Yet this does not solve the problem of 'independence, authenticity and originality' that Williams is grappling with, hence not the problem of co-optation, neutralisation, and re-volution either. It merely displaces it. The ideas and values used in the forging of a critical discourse under such circumstances are neither authentic nor original. They have been borrowed from another society. The dominated may now be independent of the dominant culture of their society but only at the cost of becoming dependent on the culture of another which, in turn, is no doubt dependent on another and so on and so forth. For there is no society outside society and no culture outside culture, no original society or culture. With this, we are back to Locke's Indian philosopher, and from here it is turtles 'all the way down' or societies and cultures spinning round and round the circle.

Bourdieu's model indicates yet another source of the ideas and values necessary for the production of a critical discourse, even if it does so only implicitly by half-pointing the finger, namely, the dominant culture itself. As we have seen, a critical discourse can emerge only where the subjective and objective structures are no longer compatible. We have interpreted this to mean a conflict between the expectations that people have and the objective possibilities for their fulfilment, and this is in line with Bourdieu's usage of these terms.[1] In his discussion of emancipation Bauman (2000: 17) has something similar to say: 'Feeling free ... to act on one's wishes, means reaching a balance between the wishes, the imagination and the ability to act... Once the balance is achieved, and as long as it stays intact, "liberation" is a meaningless slogan, lacking motivational force.' If we bracket off a deus ex machina and the case of cultural contact that we have already discussed, what remains is the dominant culture of one's own society. The expectations people have can only be those that their society generated and encouraged them to have. This, in a nutshell, is the argument that James Scott develops in his critical discussion of hegemony – that the source of discord and critique is the dominant culture itself. As we have seen, Williams says something of a similar nature: '[T]he dominant culture, so to say, at once produces and limits its own forms of counter-culture.' Yet Williams's argument is hesitant and hypothetical – 'so to say' – and, in any case, remains undeveloped.

There is a gap, Scott says, echoing Bourdieu, Bauman, and, in a certain sense, Derrida, between what the dominant culture promises and what it can actually deliver – between preaching and doing, as we have seen in the discussion on the postcolonial. And this gap exists, Scott goes on to say drawing on Marx, because, as the latter points out in *The German Ideology*, the ruling ideas are precisely an *idealised* expression of the dominant material conditions and therefore impossible to actualise. Without this gap there would be no critique. Without it, we may add following Derrida who conceptualises it as *différance*, there would be nothing:

> The crucial point is ... that the very process of attempting to legitimise a social order by idealizing it *always* provides its subjects with the means, the symbolic tools, the very ideas for a critique that operates entirely within hegemony. *For most purposes* ... it is not at all necessary for subordinate classes to set foot *outside* the confines of the ruling ideas in order to formulate a critique of power. The *most common* form of class struggle arises from the failure of a dominant ideology to live up to the implicit promises it necessarily makes. The dominant ideology can be turned against its privileged beneficiaries not only because subordinate groups develop their own interpretations, understandings, and readings of its ambiguous terms, but also because of the promises that the dominant classes must make to propagate it in the first place (Scott 1985: 338; my emphases).

It seems then, that contrary to what many still believe – contrary, that is, to the dominant ideology – one does not need to think for oneself to criticise the social order. The condition of possibility of critique is in fact the reverse. In most cases, for 'the most common forms of class struggle', one need only take the dominant ideology for granted. Being an idealised version of the possible, it is bound to fall short of what it promises to deliver and will provide in this way all the ammunition the dominated need. Paradoxically, the more one takes the dominant ideology for granted, the more likely is one to rebel against the social order it legitimises. And, reciprocally, the more one refuses to believe in what the dominant ideology promises, which is to say, the less one takes it seriously, the more likely is one to conform. We should mention in this respect Scott's perceptive comments on Paul Willis's well-known study of school counterculture in Britain. Working-class youngsters are not convinced that doing well at school will improve their chances in life. If they did, 'they would feel far more cruelly deceived later'. Thus, Scott goes on to say, Willis 'argues implicitly that *social stability and compliance* requires that the ideology of the school *fail to impress* itself on working-class youngsters. Indeed, those working-class youngsters who pose the greatest problem for school authorities enter the workforce thoroughly *cynical* but *without aspirations* that could possibly be betrayed' (Scott 1985: 338–339, n.74; my emphases). The working-class youngsters refuse to take the dominant ideology for granted; they do not believe in it and expect little from society; they become cynical, but because they have no aspirations that could be betrayed, they pose no threat to the system. We may say, as Bauman says, that for them liberation is a 'meaningless slogan'.

What we see beginning to crystallise here is the collapse of another distinction, which follows the same logic as the collapse of the other distinctions we have already encountered – between giving and taking and activity and receptivity – and has the same cause – the impossibility of presence. We are beginning to see that there is nothing to separate resistance from conformity, that the two fuse together and become interchangeable. What Scott is saying without quite saying it or, at any rate, what he is interpreting Willis to be saying, is that resistance (activity) amounts to the same thing as conformity (receptivity) and conformity to the same thing as resistance. Those who resist the social order, much like those who resist the global order dominated by Europe, are precisely those who have taken its promises for granted as a grant or gift – which is not a gift, but as far as they are concerned ought to be. And those who conform to it, the working-class youngsters in this case, have arrived to the point of conformity by way of a prior resistance, by rejecting this gift as a phantom and refusing to engage in the giving and taking. We shall return to this argument in the last chapter.

We have already dealt with the impossibility of the outside, but we must nonetheless reiterate the argument here, even if briefly, because the outside is implicit in what Scott says in the quotation above. Although he does not elaborate, one presumes that he is referring to the least, rather than the 'most common forms of class struggle', the most revolutionary struggles perhaps, those occasions when 'modern revolutions become serious', as Marx (1963 [1862]: 19) says in *The Eighteenth Brumaire*. The implication of what Scott says is that for such struggles it may be necessary to step outside the dominant ideology and draw inspiration from elsewhere. There are no such struggles, however. All begin on the inside and are inspired by the inside and what goes on in it, whether the inside is one's own society or another. And because they do, they also end up on the inside – at the very point where they began. For the European revolutionaries of the nineteenth century, in any case, there was no possibility of setting foot outside European culture in another sense. There was no outside worthy of consideration. As Marx and Engels point out in the *Manifesto of the Communist Party*, 'the bourgeoisie, historically, has played *a most* revolutionary part' (1978 [1848]: 475; my emphasis). Its revolutions may have hidden from its own eyes the true content of its struggle, may have forgotten the spirit of the revolution, and supplanted Habakkuk with Locke, but despite all their limitations they completed the 'task of their time'. Part of this task, Marx will argue, was the civilising of barbarians and semi-barbarians and the rescuing of idiots from themselves:

> The bourgeoisie, by the rapid improvement of all instruments of production, by the immensely facilitated means of communication, drew all, even the most *barbarian* nations into *civilisation*.... It has created enormous cities ... and has thus rescued a considerable part of the population from the *idiocy* of rural life. Just as it has made the country dependent on the towns, so it has made *barbarian and semi-barbarian* countries dependent on the civilised ones (Marx and Engels 1978: 477; my emphases).

There was nothing outside the dominant European culture, then, that could inspire the revolutionaries of the nineteenth century. Everything was within. After all, the bourgeoisie played if not *the most*, '*a most* revolutionary part' in history – apparently Marx reserved 'the most' for the proletarian revolutions themselves. All the revolutionaries of the nineteenth century needed to do to become revolutionaries was to take the bourgeois ideology of freedom, equality and the brotherhood of 'man' for granted. This is all, all revolutions and all lesser practices – rebellions, critiques, resistances – need to do.[2] The mystique surrounding such practices notwithstanding, it is conformity to the dominant culture that makes them possible. Such is the paradox – and no doubt the embarrassment.

Identity Politics

Identity politics, or the politics of recognition, is the stage on which the spectacle of political economy is currently orchestrated and performed. More than anywhere else, it is here that that the dominant ideology of enlightened humanism has been taken for granted as the grant or gift of modernity and the question of autonomy through rational reflection urgently and often agonisingly posed. And it is here too that hopes have been more visibly and tangibly frustrated. As we have seen, more than half a century after the end of colonialism and the European gift has not materialised and is yet to become (a) present in the postcolonies. Similarly, more than four decades of second-wave feminism and black activism and the dream of recognition remains as elusive as ever. And this is despite the fact that the recognition sought in all these, and other similar cases is no longer denied in practice, certainly not institutionally and not routinely, and the fact that when it is denied in theory, it is often unintentionally.

We have already noted how a book title like *The Cultural Logic of Late Capitalism* can be interpreted as an implicit affirmation of Western cultural superiority and frustrate the postcolonial critic's desire for recognition. One could no doubt multiply such examples to take into account other forms of othering. One could also refer to even more 'devilish' cases, paradoxical situations where even though the terms of address used are intentionally cast in such a way as to avoid othering, they nonetheless do little more than to confirm it as if they are following their own logic and are beyond the speaker's control. 'We learn', says Zizek in a related discussion and by way of summarising this point, 'that "fat", "stupid", "shortsighted" ... is to be replaced by "weight-challenged", etc.'. The problem with politically correct speech, he goes on to say, is that 'this censoring activity itself, by a kind of *devilish* dialectical *reversal*, starts to participate in what it purports to censor and fight ... one adds insult to injury, as it were, by the supplementary polite patronizing dimension' (Zizek 2000: 254; my emphases). We shall not multiply such examples here. We will simply state the general principle of their intelligibility. There can be no encounter of another that is not an othering. The mere act of representing someone is an act of making different – for how else can one even begin to think and talk about another if that other is not conceptualised as other but the same? This is to say also that the moment of encountering another as it truly is, in this context the same as the self, is indefinitely postponed – which is not to suggest that this other or the self can ever encounter and hence know itself as itself. As we have seen in our discussion of time, there is no such moment. The moment of encounter, of being present to oneself and in the presence of another as oneself is either always in the future and has not arrived yet or has always already arrived and is in the past. Hence, the need to *re-present* – a poor but the only available alternative – to make present what by definition has never been, and will never be, present. The reader will no doubt recognise here the structure of what Derrida calls *différance*. As we are dealing here with the social and the political rather than the epistemological, and as Derrida himself makes much of the idea of justice, even as he knows better than anyone else that there is no such thing, we will call this difference or othering *injustice*.

In identity politics and, as we have seen, in the more culturally sensitive politics of class struggle, the circle of political economy is both recognised and denied at the same time. The existence of the circle is often acknowledged, if not by everyone involved, certainly by some of the more theoretically sophisticated and analytically astute scholars. And so are the consequences of being trapped in it. 'We suffer from a contemporary "disenchantment of the world"', says Brown (1995: 26), 'more vivid than Weber let alone Marx ever imagined. This is not so much *nihilism* [my emphasis] – the oxymoronic belief in meaninglessness – as barely masked *despair* [my emphasis] about the meanings and events that humans *have* generated.' I have highlighted *despair* because it is a theme we will encounter below in our discussion of postcolonial criticism (if that is what it is). I have also highlighted Brown's point that the condition she describes is not nihilism, a desire for meaninglessness. Apparently, no one wants to live in a meaningless world, and if the modernist subject does, this is because of the events that humans themselves have generated. Which brings us back to the point with which we began – that although the circle and its consequences are often acknowledged, no one seems prepared to recognise the finality of it all, the fact that there is no exit to the circle. If it is humans who created this circle, the modernist subject reasons, humans should also be able to eliminate it. Hence all the strategies employed to keep the vision of autonomy alive – from simple denials and embarrassing reversals to refusals to identify the 'content' of the struggle and the identity of the struggling subject. 'What if it were possible to incite a slight shift in the character of political expression and political claims common to much politicised identity?' asks Brown. Having identified revenge, or *ressentiment*, in Nietzschean terms, as the motivational force in identity politics and the cause of re-volution – not surprisingly, as this politics, like all politics, is always tied to the hegemonic – she wonders, reasonably enough, whether the situation may not be reversible:

> What if we sought to supplant the language of 'I am' – with its defensive closure on identity, its insistence on the fixity of position, its equation of social with moral positioning – with the language of 'I want this for us'? ... What if we were to rehabilitate the memory of desire within identificatory process, the moment in desire – either 'to have' or 'to be' – *prior to its wounding*? [my emphasis]. ... If every 'I am' is something of a resolution of the movement of desire into *fixed* and *sovereign identity* [my emphases], then this project might involve not only learning to speak but to *read* 'I am' in this way: as potentially in motion, as temporal, as *not-I* [my emphasis], as deconstructable according to a genealogy of want rather than as fixed interests or experiences (Brown 1995: 75).

The shift that Brown is proposing is by no means slight; and it is by no means possible. We have already looked at a similar argument in the discussion on Marx. It is an argument about subjects who desire something – recognition – without having any reason to desire it, no wounds caused by discrimination, exclusion, humiliation, and so on. For as Brown says, the desire to be recalled in memory is a desire prior to this sort of injury, in other words, prior to misrecognition. It should be clear also that although these subjects know exactly what they want for themselves – *this* – they are not meant to know what they themselves are. They do not wish to have a fixed identity but on the contrary to transform the 'I am' into a 'not I'. What we are being asked here to take seriously as a hypothesis is the following: although these subjects do not quite recognise themselves, they nonetheless recognise that they have been misrecognised; and although they now wish to be recognised for what they are – *this* – they themselves do not wish to be anything specific – nothing fixed, closed and permanent, neither this nor that.

Of all the examples that one could assemble to demonstrate the recognition of the circle of political economy and its simultaneous denial, I shall discuss only two. The first, which takes us back to the second chapter of this book and the problem of provincializing or decentring Europe, is concerned with postcolonial identities. The second refers to gender and the politics of sexual identity. In this latter case, we will reflect on the reflections of one of the leading scholars in the area – Judith Butler.

In the first chapter of *Provincializing Europe*, also published previously as an article, the postcolonial critic sets out to explain the nature of his project by indicating what it is *not*. (Let us recall here that the same tactic was used in the last paragraph of the last chapter). The project, the postcolonial critic says, 'does not call for a *simplistic, out-of-hand* rejection of modernity, liberal values, universals, science, reason, grand narratives, totalizing explanations, and so on' (2000: 42; my emphases). Could it be that it calls for a complex rejection, a rejection not 'out of hand' but one that gives with one hand and takes or keeps with the other? We have argued that this is what it strives to do – embrace European thought as a gift, but at the same time reject it as an insult or poison. We have also argued that because it strives to do the impossible, it is not, neither the one nor the other – hence *not* a project of any sort. The postcolonial critic accounts for the identification of his 'project' in the negative – in terms of what it is not – differently. It has not been written yet, he says. 'The project of provincializing "Europe" refers to a history that does not yet exist.' Because it does not yet exist, one cannot say what it would be like, except in a 'programmatic manner', but one can say what it will not be like, if only to 'forestall misunderstanding' (2000: 42). Programmatically then, 'the idea is to write into the history of modernity the ambivalences, contradictions, the use of force, and the strategies and ironies that attend it' (2000: 43). This is a salutary idea, but will it constitute a project, an undertaking that will achieve certain concrete results? Will it, in other words, make any difference whether it is undertaken or not? For once, the postcolonial critic will not mince his words, at least not initially. It is impossible to provincialize Europe, he will admit, and the only thing left for anyone who cares to undertake such a job is the despair of a politics that goes round and round in circles:

And, finally – since 'Europe' cannot after all be provincialized within the institutional site of the university whose knowledge protocols will *always take us back* to the terrain where all contours follow that of my hyperreal Europe – the project of provincializing Europe must realize within itself its own *impossibility*. It therefore looks to a history that embodies this politics of *despair* (2000: 45; my emphases).

Let us note, to begin with, the circularity of this undertaking. One cannot decentre Europe within the university because the knowledge protocols that it recognises as legitimate will always take one back to the point of departure – Europe as the centre of the world – the very idea that one is striving to get away from. Having taken this knowledge for granted as a grant or gift, the postcolonial critic cannot avoid giving back to Europe. Even though this may be the last thing that he wishes to do, he gives back to Europe the recognition it demands and hence gives in to it. Whatever the postcolonial critic says about Europe, its position as the centre of the world is always reflected in his discourse, and there is nothing he can do to change the reflection. Every time he tries to decentre it, he ends up recentring it – hence the despair. But what if, one might ask, postcolonial discourse sought to decentre Europe on the basis of some other form of knowledge, one that does not follow the protocols of the university, perhaps even a knowledge that comes from outside Europe? Would that not achieve something? The postcolonial critic will not even consider this as a possibility – and although it is true that it is not a possibility, our reasons for saying this and those that motivate the postcolonial critic are totally different:

> It will have been clear by now that this is not a call for cultural relativism or for *atavistic, nativist histories*. Nor is this a programme of a simple rejection of modernity, which would be, in many situations, *politically suicidal*. I ask for a history that deliberately makes visible, within the very structure of its narrative forms, its own repressive strategies and practices, the part it plays in collusion with the narratives of citizenships in assimilating to the project of the modern state all other possibilities of human solidarity (2000: 45; my emphases).

Cultural relativism and nativist histories are excluded from the conceptual toolkit of this project. Both would be a simplistic rejection of modernity, the latter burdened with atavism as well – and, as we have noted, the postcolonial critic is striving to produce a sophisticated, complex rejection – one that embraces as it rejects. Nativist histories in particular would reject modernity out of hand, without keeping anything with the other hand – a practice that, as the postcolonial critic himself says, would be suicidal. We have noted already whose life is at stake here and we will not reiterate the argument. We will consider however the question of native discourses as an alternative to university discourse. Can they perhaps provincialize Europe? Perhaps they can, but this is not how the question should be posed. One should be asking rather whether they would be interested at all in provincializing Europe. If they have not been constituted with an eye on European history, if they are not motivated by injury and have no wounds to nurture, they would probably be indifferent to such a project. There would be little if anything at all at stake for them in an undertaking of this sort. Freedom from European domination – the stake par excellence – would probably be a 'meaningless slogan'. No doubt they could be adopted, appropriately transformed and used for such a purpose, but they would no longer be the native discourses that they were except perhaps in name. Moreover, and more importantly, if they were to be so transformed, if they were now secretly motivated by injury and 'ressentiment', they would have the fate of any other such discourse. What is to be done then?:

> The politics of despair will require of such a history [the history that has not yet been written] that it lay bare to its readers the reasons why such a predicament is *necessarily inescapable*. This is a history that will attempt the *impossible:* to look forward to its own death by tracing that which resists and escapes the best human effort at translation across cultural and other semiotic systems, so that the world may once again be imagined as radically heterogeneous (2000: 45–46; my emphases).

The 'necessarily inescapable' predicament, it should be clear, is the impossibility of decentring Europe, the inability to avoid giving in to it, the fact that even the best efforts to translate other cultures into Western culture always fail and the former always emerge as an inferior version of the latter. But if it is impossible not to give in to Europe, if all attempts to decentre it are destined to recentre it, if, in short, historicism is unavoidable, one could at least ask history to tell its readers *why* it is impossible. Such a question, consistently and persistently pursued, would probably destroy the history that answers it and perhaps silence the critic himself, but at least he and the readers will know. Yet the postcolonial critic will not even begin to write such a history. At some point between the article and the book chapter, he will make a complete reversal and deny that he knows what he knows – the impossibility. There is far too much at stake in such an undertaking it seems, too much to lose, perhaps even everything. It would be suicidal. Hence, having recognised the circle of political economy, the 'necessarily inescapable' return to the point of departure, having advocated the politics of despair with passion, the postcolonial critic will retrace his steps, hoping to find if not a clearly marked exit, then perhaps an overlooked opening:

> A postscript (1999): This chapter reproduces in an abridged form my first attempt (in 1992) at articulating the problem of provincializing Europe. This original statement remains a *point of departure* for what follows. Several of the themes broached in it ... are fleshed out in the rest of the book. But the 'politics of despair' I once proposed with some *passion* do not any longer drive the larger argument presented here (2000: 46; my emphases).

The article of 1992 and the version that appears as the first chapter of the book have the same point of departure. For both the aim is to decentre European thought. They also have the same point of arrival, which is the point of departure. Both go round and come round. Apart from the abridgment, the difference between the two is that former recognises the circle and despairs, whereas the latter refuses to accept its finality and breathes a sigh of relief. The postcolonial critic as a modernist subject does not need to look forward to its death as such a subject. It can now buy more time – but at what cost? – forget about death, perhaps even pretend that it will live forever.

For the second example of the attitude that recognises the existence of the circle but refuses to accept its finality, I will turn to Judith Butler's reflections on *The Psychic Life of Power*. As she points out in the opening pages of the book, power is usually understood as something pressing on the subject from the outside, thereby preventing it from doing what it wishes to do or coercing it into doing things that it does not wish to do. We might call this the liberal conception of power because in this tradition liberty is broadly understood and noninterference by others.[3] We are all familiar with this sort of power, Butler goes on to say, but neither the concept nor the experience exhaust what power is and what it does. If one were to follow Foucault, one would arrive at a very different understanding of power:

> If, following Foucault, we understand power as *forming* the subject as well, as providing the very conditions of its existence and the trajectory of its desire, then power is not simply what we oppose but also, in a strong sense, what we depend on for our existence and what we harbor and preserve in the beings that we are.... Are there not discursive conditions for the articulation of any 'we'? Subjection consists precisely in this fundamental dependency on a discourse we never chose but that, paradoxically, initiates and sustains our agency (Butler 1997: 2).

The discourse on which the subject depends, which names any individual or collective identity, is what it has taken for granted and hence what makes it the subject that it is. As Foucault himself (1987: 11) says, it is the 'patterns that he [the subject] finds in the culture and which are proposed, suggested and imposed on him by his culture, his society and his social group'. Let us note here in passing that in his discussion on Foucault's understanding of power, Lukes (2005: 97) notes, not without a certain satisfaction, that with this answer to the question of what it means to say that power constitutes the subject 'the ultra-radicalism of Foucault's view of power dissolves. For it amounts to restating some elementary sociological commonplaces'. Lukes goes on to list them: 'Individuals are socialized; they are oriented to roles and practices that are culturally and socially given; they internalize these and may experience them as freely chosen; indeed, their freedom may, as Durkheim liked to say, be the fruit of regulation – the outcome of disciplines and controls.' We are not concerned here with Foucault's presumed radicalism, but Lukes is no doubt right in pointing out the sociological basis of Foucault's argument. The issue that concerns us is the implications of this understanding of power, however sociologically commonplace it might be. If it is a question of taking, as everyone seems to agree, it is also a question of giving (in and up). If it is power that makes the subject what it is, everything that the subject does, including resisting power, presupposes and reproduces it. The subject can do nothing to escape power. Whatever it does always already comes back to confirm it in its dominated position. Having taken from power – nothing less than one's conditions of existence and trajectory of one's desire, everything in other words – the subject cannot avoid giving in to it no matter how hard it tries. Butler is well aware of this circularity. 'Such a formulation', she says, 'suggests that in the act of opposing subordination, the subject reiterates its subjection (a notion shared by both psychoanalysis and Foucauldian accounts' (1997: 12). But perhaps things are not as bleak as they appear in this scenario. Perhaps luck, if not anything else, is still on the subject's side. Butler certainly likes to think so:

> The double aspect of subjection [being both an agent and a subject] appears to lead to a *vicious circle*: the agency of the subject appears to be an effect of its subordination. Any effort to oppose that subordination will necessarily presuppose and reinvoke it. *Luckily*, the story survives this impasse.... Power considered as a condition of the subject is necessarily *not* the same as power considered as what the subject is said to wield. A significant and potentially enabling reversal occurs when power shifts from its status as a condition of agency to the subject's 'own' agency (constituting an *appearance* of power in which the subject *appears* as the condition of its 'own' power) (Butler 1997: 12; my emphases).

It seems that something significant happens at a certain moment in this process, an instant of transmutation, or transubstantiation, perhaps – but if so it cannot be anything that happens *in* time. This is the moment when power changes its substance and from being the condition of possibility agency it becomes agency itself. At that moment, power appears – seems like, or emerges and becomes (a) present? – as the subject's own power rather than the power that makes it subject. Is this a story with a happy ending then? Does the subject, against all odds and before it despairs completely, overcome the obstacles that separate it from itself so that in the end, and at the end, is reunited with it in a passionate embrace? Not quite. For although the vicious circle only appears to be a vicious circle, although the subject's agency only appears to be an effect of its subordination, these appearances appear to be more than appearances. They seem to have some sort of substance. And the other way round: the appearance of power as the effect of the subject rather than its cause seems to have no substance, to be only an appearance. As Butler goes on to say, '[T]his conclusion' – the conclusion, in other words, that power as agency is not the same as the power that makes agency possible – 'is not to be thought of as (a) a resistance that is *really* a recuperation of power or (b) a recuperation that is *really* a resistance. It is both at once, and this ambivalence forms the bind of agency' (1997:13). Butler uses the term *ambivalence* to describe this bind, but *contradiction* is surely the more appropriate term. For what she seems to be saying is that resistance is both a recuperation of power and not a recuperation of power and, reciprocally, that recuperation of power is both resistance to power and not resistance to power – or, put in another way, that resistance is both resistance and not resistance, recuperation of power both recuperation and not recuperation.

The laborious manoeuvring to escape the circle, this going round and round in circles – which is the most striking characteristic of Butler's text – will continue unabated, but here we will look at one final example. The 'larger cultural and political predicament' of our time, Butler says, is 'how to *take* an oppositional relation to power that is, admittedly, implicated in the very power that one opposes' [my emphasis]. Can the subject take without giving (in and up)? Can it really oppose the power in which it is implicated? Yes and no, Butler will say:

> Often this *postliberatory* insight has led to the conclusion that all agency here meets its *impasse*.... I would suggest that no historical or logical conclusions follow *necessarily* from this primary complicity with subordination, but that some possibilities tentatively do. That agency is implicated in subordination is not the sign of a *fatal self-contradiction* at the core of the subject.... But neither does it restore a *pristine* notion of the subject, derived from some classical liberal-humanist formulation, whose agency is always and only opposed to power. The first view characterises politically sanctimonious form of fatalism; the second, naive form of political optimism. I hope to steer clear of both these alternatives (1997: 17; my emphases).

Let us begin with the way in which Butler describes the insight we have been discussing – postliberatory. Although she does not explain what she means by this term, it cannot possibly be 'after liberation', for what is at stake in the insight is precisely the prospect of liberation. We shall take it to be a grudging recognition that the subject is beyond liberation – grudging because in the very same sentence Butler will retract it. One is not to conclude from this insight that the subject has reached an impasse, says Butler. It does not follow either historically or logically or, at least, it does not follow necessarily. The subject may have reached an impasse, but it may have not. Because there is no historical or logical necessity, no one can be certain. The manoeuvring continues. That the subject is implicated in its own domination is not a sign of self-contradiction at the core of the subject or, at least, not a fatal one. It is a self-contradiction but one that the subject can live with. It simply means that the subject is no longer pristine, that it has been compromised by power. But perhaps this too is not a necessary conclusion, because, as Butler will go on to say, 'the subject exceeds the logic of contradiction, is an excrescence of logic, as it were' (1997: 17). If the subject exceeds the logic of contradiction, then logically this logic does not apply to it. But if it does not apply, it makes no sense to say what Butlers asserts – that there is a self-contradiction at the core of the subject, even if not fatal – and it *does* make sense to say what she denies – that the subject is pristine. Butler, in any case, will go on to retract this claim. It seems that the subject is subject to the logic of contradiction after all: '[T]o claim that the subject exceeds either/or is not to claim that it lives in some free zone of its own making'. If the subject could step outside the circle that encircles it, it would be able to create such a free zone – from scratch, *ex nihilo*, without the need to take anything from anyone and hence without the need to give in to anyone. But it cannot create such a pristine zone. Exceeding, Butler will go on to say, 'is not escaping, and the subject exceeds precisely that to which it is bound' (1997: 17).

To round up the discussion, let us turn briefly to how the contradiction with which Butler has been struggling – in a nutshell, the idea of the subjugated agent – could possibly be avoided. We have already noted that Kant dealt with same contradiction by positioning two subjects or two aspects of the subject, one empirical, the other noumenal. The former is subject to causation and cannot be free, the latter a product of the mind, the subject as a thing in itself, and freedom is its essence. The former is what can be experienced, the latter a figment of the imagination – a phantom. Butler does not seem prepared to accept Kant's solution. She does not want to be a 'sanctimonious fatalist' but nor does she want to be a 'naive optimist'. She wants neither the one nor the other. She wants to be somewhere in the middle – between and betwixt – partly pessimistic and partly optimistic. In short, she wants to maintain a liminal position. If so the discourse of the feminist critic, much like that of the postcolonial critic, is bound to remain contradictory and inarticulate.

The economy we have been discussing in this chapter undercuts any practical political programme whose aim is to liberate the modernist subject, whether the postcolonial, gendered, sexed, or racialized subject, to mention only a few of its manifestations. 'What remains to be considered', says Butler, speaking from the sort of liminal position we have just described, is 'how we might make such a conception of the subject work as a notion of political agency in *postliberatory times*' (Butler 1997: 18; my emphasis). How, indeed? If these are postliberatory times, it is because the subject is beyond liberation. It is unclear, therefore, how this contradictory notion – the subjugated agent – can be made to work, but one possible argument could be that in a universe where the subject thinks for itself (if it does), there may still be an element of choice. If liberation per se is impossible, it may be possible for the subject to at least choose how and by whom it will be governed. This seems to be what Foucault had in mind in his discussion of the critical attitude as a peculiarly Western phenomenon. The question of how to govern, which Foucault calls *governmentality* and traces back to the fifteenth and sixteenth centuries, cannot be dissociated from the reverse question – how not to be governed:

I do not mean by this that governmentalization would be opposed, in a kind of inverted contrary affirmation, to 'We do not want be governed, and we do not want to be governed *at all.*' What I mean is that in the great anxiety surrounding the way to govern and in the inquiries into modes of governing, one detects a perpetual question, which would be: How not to be governed *like that*, by that, in the name of these principles, in view of such objectives and by the means of such methods, not like that, not for that, not by them? (Foucault 1996: 384).

That the subject will be governed in one way or another, in the name of certain principles, for some purpose and by certain means, by them or someone like or unlike them is beyond question. But the specifics of government are not cast in stone and the subject may be able to resist the more oppressive forms. Hence Foucault defines critique as 'the art of not being governed so much' (1996: 384).

We will not dispute Foucault's argument either on logical or empirical grounds. We will examine, rather, the assumptions on which it is based. The problem with the argument is that it no longer refers to the kind of power associated with his name. It is operating with the liberal conception of power, as something pressing on the subject from the outside, the kind of power that says no. If, however, following Foucault or one of his 'spectres', power does not simply say no, if it also says yes and makes things possible, if it forms the subject by 'providing the very conditions of its existence and the trajectory of its desire', then the subject has no choice. It does not choose how or by whom it is to be governed any more than how or by whom it is not to be governed, neither the power that dominates it nor the specific object of its critique. On the contrary, it is chosen by them. The very desire not to be governed 'like that, by that, not for that' and so on is by Foucault's own definition a product of power or, let us say recalling Lukes's sociological point, the product of one's society and culture. Giving in to this desire, therefore, means nothing else than conforming to the dominant ideology of one's society and culture, namely, the idea of autonomy. This is to say that to be aware of one's domination and to desire not to be governed in a particular way is to be unaware of one's domination. It is to conform to the dominant ideology at a deeper level than that of immediate awareness, and to get to this level it is necessary to carry out the kind of analysis that Foucault has carried out in his various projects. Thus critique cannot be 'the art of voluntary inservitude, of reflective indocility', as Foucault (1996: 386) says in the same essay. If it is, one is operating with the assumptions of the liberal conception of power which is blind to the more profound conformity that renders ideas of 'voluntary inservitude' and 'reflexive indocility' possible to begin with it.

But enough has been said to substantiate the point with which we began, namely, that the circle of political economy is both recognised and denied in the desperate attempt of the modernist subject to find an exit. Yet there is no exit. No matter how much the subject refuses to take – on trust, for granted – it has always already taken and lives on borrowed time. And because it has always already taken, it has always already given in to power, always already conformed to it.

It should be clear that the economy we have been discussing in this chapter – the political – is an extension or another version of the economy of gift exchange and the economy of thought and operates with the same logic. If nothing is free in the economy of gift exchange, not to speak of the market economy, no one can be free either, whether epistemologically free – free of bias and therefore objective – or politically free, namely, autonomous. If giving is the same as taking, if everything that the subject gives returns in one form of another and everything that it says about the world refers back to it as the locus from which the world is perceived, if, in short, the subject is inescapably subjective, then it is also and as inescapably subjugated. This is another cost of living, the price that one has to pay for being a political being.

Notes

1. See, for example Bourdieu (1990).

2. Elsewhere (Argyrou 2002, 2005), I argued there is not a single critical contemporary discourse – whether feminism, anti-racism, or postcolonialism, to mention only the major ones – that does not aspire to the bourgeois ideology of Enlightenment humanism. This ideology is their very condition of possibility (and impossibility).

3. For example, Mill (1991 [1859]: 17): 'The only freedom which deserves the name, is that of pursuing our own good in our own way, so long as we do not attempt to deprive others of theirs, or impede their effort to obtain it.'

CHAPTER 5

THE COST OF LIVING

Thinking and Not Thinking

In the third chapter of this book I have argued that what the motto of the Enlightenment prescribes – 'think for yourself' – is impossible and that this impossibility is precisely the impossibility of making (a) present, which includes making oneself (a) present to oneself. The point was argued primarily in terms of the historical unconscious, that is, with respect to what the subject takes for granted in time or in the meantime to become a subject – a self-identifying and identifiable being, a member of a particular society and culture and so on. As we noted, the philosophers of the Enlightenment had no conception of a historical unconscious in the sociological sense. They operated with the assumption of an always already fully formed subject that takes for granted because of laziness and cowardice or, at any rate, because it is persuaded to take at the discursive level. In this chapter we will put the historical unconscious aside and return to the intellectual milieu of the Enlightenment. We will note, to begin with, what seem to have eluded the protagonists of the Enlightenment, which is also what deluded them, namely, that the motto itself is precisely an example of taking for granted. And we will argue that even if this was the only thing that the subject had ever had to take for granted to think for itself, it would still not be thinking for itself. The object of this exercise is partly to meet the protagonists of the Enlightenment on their own ground and partly to highlight the role of time in this impossibility. It takes a little more than an instant for the motto of the Enlightenment to be perceived and recognised as a gift of thought. At that very moment it becomes untenable.

Let us recall, to begin with, one of the first critiques of Kant's famous essay on the Enlightenment, namely, Hamann's disagreement as to whom should be blamed for the general state of immaturity in which Kant and other luminaries regarded their time and society to be. Kant blamed the immature; Hamann, the self-appointed guardians. For Kant immaturity was self-incurred, something that people brought upon themselves by being unwilling to think for themselves. For Hamann the reverse was the case. It was because certain people – Kant, for example – took it upon themselves to tell others how they ought to lead their lives that people were rendered immature. Without self-appointed guardians, the problem would not exist. Hamann's line of reasoning is not wrong but neither is it entirely right. If immaturity is a function of the presence of self-appointed guardians, it is equally the case that there can be no guardians without the presence of subjects receptive to the idea of being guided. The relationship is reciprocal, a case of complicity between guardians and the guided. More to the point, however, the apportioning of blame to either the guardians or the immature is appropriate and works only at a certain level of analysis, the most obvious and less significant at that – the level of willing or unwilling subjects. As we have noted in the previous chapter, however, this is a structural condition that follows its own logic irrespective of subjective wishes and desires.

Perhaps we will never know if Kant secretly entertained the desire to become the guardian of what he considered as the unthinking masses, which, let us note in passing, included 'the entire fair sex' (Kant 1991: 54). For the purposes of the present discussion, however, it makes no difference that we do not know. Whether he wished it or not, whether he liked it or not, it was impossible for him not to become one and hence undercut in this way the very thing he sought to promote. Kant gave his contemporaries a gift of thought, and because he did, he could not avoid taking something in return irrespective of whether he wanted to take anything or not – their recognition, for example (and no doubt ours), or the satisfaction that in this way he was making a contribution to what he considered a worthwhile cause, namely, society's enlightenment. For why bother encouraging others to think for themselves if there was nothing to be gained from it, even if what was there to be gained was nothing more than confirmation of one's vision of the world? By confirming himself in this way, namely, as someone who knew what it meant to be enlightened and why it mattered, by thinking on behalf of the immature about such matters hence appointing himself as their guardian, Kant confirmed also the impossibility of what he considered not only possible but also 'almost inevitable' (1991:55). He demonstrated – unwittingly, unwillingly but inevitably – that an enlightened society, which is to say as Kant himself said, a society whose members thought for themselves and led their lives without the guidance of others is impossible. The only way he could abolish guardianship was by becoming guardian himself. The only way he could construct an enlightened society was by undermining the foundations on which it was supposed to be constructed. Such is the paradox. It is the paradox of taking while giving even when what one really wishes to do is to give, not to take – the impossibility of making (a) present, in this case, an enlightened society. There can be no such society, as we have said. It can only be anticipated in a future that will never come and become (a) present or remembered as being present in a past that never was (a) present, in short, it can be represented but never experienced. It is a figment of the modernist imagination, a fantasy or a phantom – which, of course, is not to be criticised per se. If there is anything to be criticised, this is the pretention that the phantom is a real living being, and no doubt also the critique of other people's phantoms for being phantoms.

Let us now turn to the other side of the equation, all those presumed not to be thinking for themselves and therefore in need of enlightenment. What are they to do in the face of such generosity? Should they accept this gift of enlightenment, take it on trust, for granted, as it is granted, or should they refuse it as the motto of the Enlightenment itself says they should? Once again, it makes no difference what they should to do, what they wish to do, or what they finally decide to do. For they have no choice in the matter. No matter what they do, they will never become enlightened. If they refuse this gift, they would perhaps be thinking for themselves, at least insofar as they would be refusing to accept the guidance of another as Kant prescribed. Yet although they may be thinking for themselves in this sense, they would not be thinking for themselves. They would be refusing to accept precisely the directive that they ought to be thinking for themselves. In other words, they would be thinking for themselves for the express purpose of not thinking for themselves. What we see emerging here, then, is a paradox whereby thinking for oneself becomes the very basis of not thinking for oneself. The same paradox haunts the second choice, if that is what it is. If the immature were to accept the gift of enlightenment, if they were to take it for granted, they would obviously not be thinking for themselves. They would be acting under the guidance of another. Although their purpose would no doubt be to begin thinking for themselves, to begin they should not begin. They should not think for themselves to think for themselves. The condition of possibility of thinking for oneself becomes its reverse – not thinking for oneself. But what if, one might object, the immature do not refuse this gift and do not take it for granted either – neither the one nor the other? What if they accept it only after careful consideration, after they have used their own understanding and found it a worthwhile idea to accept? This, it could be argued, would surely overcome the problem that we are presenting here as insurmountable. But it does not. An objection of this sort presumes enlightened subjects before enlightenment, which, if they were perceived to exist, would render the Enlightenment redundant.

Any way one looks at it then, the subject of the Enlightenment will never become enlightened. If it refuses its gift, it would remain unenlightened. If it takes it for granted, it would also remain unenlightened. With this, we have reached the point where the distinction between thinking for oneself and not thinking for oneself collapses and is no longer possible to keep the two apart. They become the same, in the same way and for the same reasons that giving is the same as taking and taking the same as giving. Thinking for oneself or *giving* oneself the gift of thought – an auto-gift, as we have said – becomes the same thing as not thinking for oneself, the same as *taking* this gift from another. The pretensions of the Enlightenment aside, there is no such thing as thinking for oneself.

One of the immediate consequences of the collapse of the distinction between thinking for oneself and taking for granted is the rehabilitation of the ordinary understanding of what it means to think for oneself. If it means making a judgement and taking a decision, then there is no one who does not think for oneself. Even the person who relies totally on the judgement of another – someone, say, who believes that birth control is wrong simply because the Pope said it is wrong – even such a person is thinking for itself. She – this hypothetical person – decides to trust the Pope and not some other authority, hence, she is making a judgement. If 'she trusted the Pope', says Bittner in his critical discussion of Kant's essay on enlightenment, 'she did not therefore fail to use her own understanding. It takes understanding to accept the pronouncements of an authority'. It no doubt does. For Bittner, therefore, thinking for oneself, 'an idea of which Kant, together with many if his contemporaries, tried to make a great deal, is a *triviality*: to be thinking at all, however excessively relying on others' judgment is to be thinking for oneself' (1996: 348; my emphasis). Yet, having made this argument, Bittner is not about to eliminate the dichotomy altogether, and because what he has to say further comes to bear on the argument we have tried to develop in this book, we shall pursue it further ourselves.

For Bittner everyone thinks for themselves, even those who are guided by another, but this does not mean that everyone is guided by another. Some people, it seems, are capable of guiding themselves and will not allow anyone to guide them, at least not in all circumstances. Thus, although Bittner eliminates the dichotomy between thinking for oneself and taking for granted, he does so only to reproduce it in another form or on another register – that of being and not being guided by another. Hence the argument: 'Being guided and not being guided by another are two ways of using one's understanding, one *correct* and the other *incorrect*' (Bittner 1996: 348; my emphases). What Bittner gives with one hand then – the recognition that everyone thinks for themselves – he takes with the other – by setting up the distinction between the correct and the incorrect way of thinking for oneself. But with this, he renders his own critique of Kant trivial. Although his dichotomy is between different ways of thinking for oneself, the criterion he uses to set it up is exactly the same criterion that Kant used to set up the dichotomy between thinking for oneself and taking for granted – the guidance of another. If one is guided, one is not thinking for oneself correctly (Bittner) or not thinking for oneself at all (Kant). The guided subject is acting incorrectly according to Bittner, immaturely according to Kant. Not that there is no difference between being wrong and being immature. In the present context however, it becomes trivial because what is at stake in both cases is the same thing – dependence on another. Whether this dependence is conceptualised as the result of not thinking for oneself correctly (which can be corrected) or not thinking for oneself at all (which can also be corrected) is at the end of the day immaterial. The dependent subject needs to be corrected and will presumably be corrected by those who know what it means to be correct – the enlighteners, as Bittner will call them later in his essay. We must, therefore, ask what this correct way of being is and whether it is possible at all.

For Bittner enlightenment is not simply a question of not being guided by another – *any other*. It is a question of not being guided by another who is believed to be higher. As we shall see shortly, Bittner uses several terms to explain what he means by *higher:* sacred, sublime, celestial, noble, worthy of respect. Higher, then, may be another word for transcendental, something unconditioned by the empirical, hence also pure. If so there is no doubt that this is also what Kant himself meant by guidance – guidance by a higher authority – and as we shall see, Bittner will come to recognise this in the end. Kant's most important critique, after all, is precisely an example of the refusal to be guided by those who claimed to possess 'pure reason' and could, therefore, confidently pronounce on such issues as the existence of God or the immortality of the soul. Having said this, and as we have noted in the third chapter, it is also the case that Kant's badly chosen examples of immaturity could be read as saying, guided not only by something or someone higher but by any other – a doctor, for example, concerning one's diet. This is how Bittner reads Kant's essay, and to make his point he uses the example of an accountant. Being guided by an accountant when it comes to one's tax returns does not mean that one is unenlightened. Being guided by the Pope, on the other hand – Bittner's other example – means precisely this, even if one is still thinking for oneself. Unlike accountants, the Pope is believed to be himself or believed to be representative of a higher, transcendental authority. For Bittner, then, 'the mark of Enlightenment thought in general' is the refusal to recognise higher authorities, the attempt to show that what appears as 'high is only a particular instance of what is low':

> Enlightenment, then, gains or communicates an understanding that finds the ordinary in the *sublime*, reduces the sacred to the profane, or proves the noble *unworthy of respect.* ... *Wrongly* to believe of something that it is noble, celestial, or sublime may be called *superstition*, in an extended sense: *one can be superstitious not only in matters of religion but in art, politics, and history as well.* Thus enlightenment is an understanding that subverts superstition of all kinds. With this Kant agrees after all: 'Liberation form superstition is called enlightenment', he wrote a few years later [in the *Critique of Judgment*] (Bittner 1996: 351; my emphases).

This is probably an accurate description of what enlightenment would be if it could exist. In one word, which is Bittner's own word, it would be *desecration*.[1] We have argued that it cannot exist because guidance by another is unavoidable. We shall reiterate the argument here taking into account Bittner's qualification –

'guidance by another who is higher'. We shall assume that Bittner's defence of the Enlightenment is not auto-directed, that he himself is guided by another, even though we will not ask by *whom* specifically, whether, that is, it is by such and such an individual or collectivity. In his essay Bittner provides something of an answer himself by referring approvingly to several philosophers – Hobbes, Spinoza, and Voltaire – but one could, of course, also say that he is being guided by his own culture – and that, too, would not be an inaccurate description. What we will ask then, is not by whom but by *what* he is guided in his defence of the Enlightenment because this is what ultimately matters, not who speaks for it. We shall also ask whether it – the guide – does not fall under Bittner's category of higher, sacred, sublime, noble, and so on or, to put it in another way but still in Bittner's terms, whether it itself is not a superstition – in an 'extended sense' of the term, to be sure. It is not hard to imagine what it might be, but Bittner spells it out for us anyway. It is freedom, he says in the last section of his essay. This is what recommends the Enlightenment and guides not only Bittner but every modernist subject:

> What enlightenment in particular promises is an *open world: freedom*. The ordinary things to which the *enlightener* reduces the *false* sublime present no barriers in principle to human action and to human understanding. Here, if anywhere, we are at home, it is our *field*, and we can *move freely*.... If this is the fruit of enlightenment, how can anyone fail to be convinced and to join the endeavor? It is because moving freely is appreciated only by those who learned to enjoy their movements, and this *joy does not grow well under the shadow of what is above us* (Bittner 1996: 357; my emphases).

We shall not be concerned with the fundamental problem implicitly raised by the last two sentences of this quotation: the failure to be convinced and to join the endeavour. It is well known that this failure is often corrected by enlighteners though imposition, coercion, and force – examples of this practice are far too numerous and far too obvious to mention here. We shall simply note the paradox of a freedom enforced as another indication of its impossibility and concur with Bittner's observation: '[J]oy does not grow well under the shadow of what is above us.' Let us now turn to Bittner's criteria of the *high*. It seems unlikely that he would disagree with the proposition that freedom is a noble idea and hence worthy of respect. Perhaps he would not disagree either that there is something of the sublime about it. As for sacred, this may be more controversial, but the difference could turn out to be a matter of semantics rather than substance. If the notion of superstition can be used in an extended sense, then perhaps the notion of the sacred can be likewise extended. We shall follow Durkheim's own definition of sacred things, namely, things set apart and forbidden – set apart from ordinary things because they are extraordinary, and forbidden because they must be protected from profanation at all costs. If sacred things are profaned, Durkheim notes, their violation causes moral outrage. In this extended sense then, Bittner may agree that freedom is an example of a sacred thing. For is it not set aside and protected institutionally and constitutionally? And does not its violation cause moral outrage? It certainly does, and examples are far too common to mention here. What he would no doubt disagree with is that freedom is also an example of superstition, something that, as he says, is wrongly believed to be noble, sublime, sacred, and so on or, as in the last quotation, something that is false. But how are these terms – *wrong* and *false* – to be understood? What does Bittner mean by them? In ordinary language as much as in academic discourse something is true or right because it is an accurate representation of reality. If, therefore, to return to the example with the Pope, trusting him is an incorrect way of using one's understanding, it can only be because he is inaccurately represented as the representative of a higher authority. And this is inaccurate, one presumes by the drift of Bittner's argument, because this higher authority does not exist. It may exist as a being in itself, but we will never know because what we can know are only phenomena, things in the empirical world, the here and now. We believe we have sufficiently demonstrated that freedom does not exist in the here and now precisely because there is no now, this instant, a present present to itself. We believe we have sufficiently demonstrated also that far from being open, a field in which the subject can move freely, the world of the modernist subject is a closed world, a circle in which it is trapped and from which it cannot escape. To believe the contrary, in the reality or possibility of freedom as Bittner clearly does, surely qualifies for an example of superstition in his own extended sense. Enlightenment, therefore, is not 'an understanding that subverts superstition of all kinds'. If it were, it would not be able to get off the ground. It would have to subvert itself. It may be an understanding but one that does not understand itself.

The Modern and the Traditional

The collapse of the distinction between thinking for oneself and not thinking has an inevitable knock-on effect on the distinction that stands next in line – that between autonomy and heteronomy, freedom and un-freedom. The latter distinction stands in line not because it comes after the former historically but because it is related to it logically, because thinking for oneself was made the condition of possibility of autonomy. It was not because people began thinking for themselves (if they ever did) that the idea of autonomy occurred to them. Rather it was because the idea of autonomy occurred to them or gave itself to them to think about, as Derrida and might say, that thinking for oneself became a stake in the scholastic struggles of the seventeenth and eighteenth centuries. It was because ordinary 'men' and the 'entire fair sex' were perceived as 'domesticated animals' and on the leash or, as Locke says, because they were reduced to 'a posture of blind credulity' so that 'they might be more easily governed by, and made useful to some sort of men' that thinking for oneself was conceived as the means of changing their lot. And to the extent that people took the Enlightenment directive to think for themselves for granted – thereby demonstrating its impossibility – it is because they too had come to conceive of themselves in this way.

It should be clear, but it may still be worthwhile to spell it out, that if thinking for oneself is the same as not thinking for oneself – in the same way and for the same reasons that giving is taking and taking giving – if, in other words, all thinking presupposes taking for granted as we have been arguing, the rest of the edifice collapses. By all good logic the distinction between autonomy and heteronomy as well as the related distinction between resistance and conformity become untenable. At the limit – not taking into account the historical unconscious – the autonomy that the subject acquires by thinking for itself is the autonomy that it gives up by giving in to this directive, the dependence generated on the ideas, the people and structures that promoted them, the social order they legitimise and so on; the resistance that it puts up to become autonomous is the conformity required to render autonomy something worth fighting for. On the basis of this logic, which no doubt is no ordinary logic but no less logical for this reason, we may even say that the more autonomous a subject is, the more securely bound, and the more revolutionary, the more conformist it is. We will make a case for this shortly. For the moment let us note the other dichotomy that turns on the distinction between thinking for oneself and taking for granted, autonomy and heteronomy – the distinction between the modern and the traditional. We have already discussed what is posited as the fundamental difference between them, and we will be brief here. It is 'wholesale reflexivity', as Giddens says, reiterating what Kant said two centuries earlier and reproducing in this way not only conventional sociological wisdom, but also philosophical, political and no doubt geopolitical – reflexivity across the board or, as Kant said, thinking for oneself 'at all times'. It is wholesale reflexivity and the wholesale autonomy that this reflexivity makes possible. It should be clear that if what has been said so far is anything to go by, this distinction has the same fate as the others and we could say that the modern becomes the same as the traditional and the traditional the same as the modern. We will not, however, rely on what has been said so far. We will try to demonstrate the identity between the two – not of the abstract notions, of course, but of the ways of life they designate – by following a different route. We will try to do so by exploring a different perspective on autonomy – a Hegelian perspective.

The argument we have been trying to develop here – that the freedom of the Enlightenment is nothing – is not necessarily new. There have been earlier soundings, even if perhaps not in these terms, and even if, as in the case we will examine, their objective was to replace the subject whose autonomy is presumed to be secured through rational reflection with another subject as fantastic and imaginary as that of the Enlightenment. This is the case of the young Hegel defending Christianity and arguing against the rationalism of his time, Hegel the synthesiser and unifier of everything, including the subject itself as we shall see shortly – as if the split that allows it to turn itself into an object of reflection is something that could be avoided, as if this split was not what it means to be subject. The question that Hegel raises in the text we shall consider is whether the subject that follows its own reason is free, as Kant claimed. We have argued above, as the limiting case of this impossibility, that to follow its own reason the subject must follow the reason of another, that it must be instructed to follow its own reason by someone else, hence that it must not follow its own reason if it is to follow its own reason. Much like Kant, Hegel takes it for granted that there is a ready-made reason capable of instructing itself to follow itself – an auto-directing reason – and locates the problem somewhere else – in the split between reason and other elements of subjectivity. For Hegel, even when the subject is not directed by another, it is still directed by an other, another sort of guardian, one from within. Hence it is still not free. Part of the subject – impulses, inclinations, desires, sentiments – is directed by another part – reason – and the only difference between this subject and the subject that is directed by another subject is that the latter has its lord outside itself. Other than that, they are both equally slaves:

> Between the Shaman of the Tungus, the European prelate who rules church and state, the Voguls, and the Puritans, on the one hand, and the man who listens to his own command of duty, on the other, the difference is not that the former make themselves slaves, while the latter is free, but that the former have their lord outside themselves, while the latter carries his lord in himself, yet at the same time is his own slave. For the particular – impulses, inclinations, pathological love, sensuous experience, or whatever else it is called – the universal is necessarily and always something alien and objective (Hegel 1971 [1907]: 211).

We shall return to the solution that Hegel proposes to close this rift and the rift between the subject and the world outside it below. Not that there is a solution. As I have already suggested, there is no subject that can be present to itself, much the say way that there is no culture that can be identical to itself. A century later Freud would argue that this split is the condition of possibility of civilisation, that civilisation emerges precisely because there is a lord within that overrules everything else. For us the significance of the quotation above at this point in the argumentation is Hegel's view of the dividing line between the inside and the outside and the dividing line that this dividing line makes possible – the line that places Tungus, Voguls, European prelates, and Puritans on one side and the subject that listens to its own reason on the other. And it is significant because it may help us think through the traditional sociological division between the modern and traditional, which is our main preoccupation here. It is clear that for

Hegel there is no distinction to be made between those who think for themselves and those who do not when it comes to the question of freedom. The subject that thinks for itself (if that is what it does) is as much a subject as the subject that does not think for itself. Hegel's intention in saying this is not to question the possibility of freedom, as we are trying to do here. It is to argue rather that it cannot be attained through the means that Kant proposed – by privileging reason at the expense of everything else. For Hegel such a subject is still a split subject, its existence not fully integrated and self-contained. Parts of its subjectivity are still dependent on other parts and as long as there are parts, whether within or without, there is no autonomy. 'Spirit', says Hegel in his lectures on Universal History, 'is *self-contained existence*. Now this is freedom, exactly. For if I am dependent, my being is referred to something else which I am not; I cannot exist independently of something external. I am free, on the contrary, when my existence depends upon myself' (1991: 17). If freedom is 'self-contained existence', and if it is the object of desire, there is obviously an urgent need to unify existence, to efface the divisions within the subject as much as the division between the subject itself and the world around it.

How can such a feat and fit be accomplished? Hegel's answer to this question is well known. It is substance made subject, absolute knowledge, the realisation that the subject and the world are one and the same thing.[2] To put it in the terms we have been using here and the terms used in a recent reiteration of this thesis that we will examine below, from this point of view autonomy can be achieved only insofar as the subject takes everything for granted, which is to say, only when it has internalised the outside completely, fully appropriated it and made it its own property. Let us note here before proceeding further that there is no question of choosing between the Hegelian and the Kantian views. As we have already noted and will discuss further below, Hegelian autonomy is as untenable as Kantian autonomy, the subject that takes everything for granted the same as the subject that takes nothing for granted, namely, an impossible subject. We will examine the Hegelian view however, and for the sake of argument presume that it has substance if only to problematize the sociological understanding of the traditional that is based on the Kantian view – in the limiting case we will examine, as a form of society where everything is taken for granted, hence a society of complete conformity. Our aim will be to show that there is no difference between these types or models of society: no difference between the Hegelian type of society – in the example that follows, a completely normalised but autonomous society – and the traditional society of the traditional sociological imagination in which normalisation is synonymous with conformity; and no difference either between these two types and the Kantian model of society where nothing is taken for granted. We will turn to an article by Nancy Frazer in which she reviews the debate between Foucault and Habermas and in which she invites the reader to imagine the following scenario:

> Imagine a perfected disciplinary society in which normalizing has becomes so omnipresent, so finely attuned, so penetrating, interiorized, and subjectified, and therefore so invisible that there is no longer and need for confessors, psychoanalysts, wardens and the like. In this fully 'panopticized' society, hierarchical, asymmetrical domination of some persons by others would have become superfluous; all would surveil [sic] and police themselves. The disciplinary norms would have become so thoroughly internalized that they would not be experienced as coming from without. The members of this society would, therefore, be autonomous. They would have appropriated the other as their own and *made substance subject* (Frazer 1985: 178; my emphasis).

Frazer has Dreyfus and Rabinow claim on Foucault's behalf that such a society would not be free and challenges them to produce another definition of freedom. As far as she is concerned – or, at any rate, as far as the persona of 'the sophisticated Habermassian humanist' through which she speaks, is concerned – 'there is no good reason to oppose such a society' (1985: 179). If the subject experiences the disciplinary norms as coming from within itself, if they are so thoroughly internalised to appear as its own creation, the subject is autonomous. That the norms come from the outside, that they have been taken for granted as a grant or gift of society is neither here nor there. The subject has appropriated them and made them its own property. Hence, by conforming to them, it conforms to itself. It would have to conform to itself even if it did not want to do so because there is no longer an other to whom it would conform. The other has now been taken over completely by the self and does not exist as other. It may have been substance, but it is now subject. What we end up with then, is Hegel's very definition of freedom – 'self-contained existence'.

For Frazer the significance of this imaginary disciplinary society is conceptual, not empirical. There is no such society in the empirical world and perhaps there will never be, but reflecting on it may help us to make better sense of what exists in the empirical world. It casts 'new light', Frazer says, 'on the humanist ideals of autonomy and reciprocity' (1985: 179). It certainly cast light, even if not necessarily new, on the difference between conformity and freedom – if there is any. And it may help us also to reflect on the long-standing sociological distinction between the modern and the traditional and the difference between them – if there is any. We may wonder then: if such a kind of society were ever to materialize and become (a) present, where would it be, at what point in time would it appear? If the oblique reference to Hegel is anything to go by – making substance subject – one would expect to find such a thoroughly disciplined and thoroughly free society at the end of history, as indeed Hegel himself claims to have found it.³ If, however, as we have been arguing, there is no end, if the end is also the beginning of another rotation of the circle, such a society could be said to have existed at what is imagined as the beginning of history. And from a certain point of view – the sociological – this is precisely what is said and how it is imagined – as the original society.

Although there are countless examples of this imaginary in the sociological literature, we will stay here with Bourdieu. 'When there is a quasi-perfect correspondence between the objective order and the subjective principles of organisation (*as in ancient societies*) [my emphases]', Bourdieu says:

> the natural and social world appears as self-evident. This experience we shall call *doxa*, so as to distinguish it from an orthodox or heterodox belief implying awareness and recognition of the possibility of different or antagonistic beliefs. Schemes of thought and perception can produce the objectivity that they produce only by producing misrecognition of the limits of the cognition that they make possible, thereby founding immediate adherence, in the doxic mode, to the world of tradition experienced as a 'natural world' and taken for granted (Bourdieu 1977: 164).

It is the traditional society of the traditional sociological imagination that Bourdieu describes here, the kind of society in which everyone conforms and which modern society is said to have displaced. Having thoroughly internalised the structures of the social world, the members of such a society do not experience them as coming from without. The structures have been transmuted into 'schemes of thought and perception' and are experienced as coming from within. As a result the social world appears natural and necessary and they conform to its demands freely. But of course – and this is the whole sociological point – the members of such as society are anything but free. Bourdieu's society of complete conformity then, is Frazer's completely normalised but autonomous society, the sociologist's doxa the same as the philosopher's 'substance made subject', the traditional the same as the modern, the beginning also the end. No doubt, the sociologist would disagree with this conclusion, but this is only because he is still operating with the Kantian understanding of how autonomy can be achieved – thinking for oneself. The philosopher would disagree with this conclusion also, but this is only because she too imagines an impossible subject. This is the subject that makes everything, including itself, (a) present to itself, that takes everything for granted, appropriates the other completely so that this other no longer exists as other. Yet, by the same token, this subject no longer exists as subject either. By appropriating the other, it itself becomes the other or, rather, because there is no longer a distinction to be made between the two, what is left after this fusion is neither the one nor the other. What is left is nothing, as Hegel himself clearly saw.

But what of the real world, one might ask? Is it not the case that when everything is said and done, people in Western societies are better off than people elsewhere in the world? Even a 'utilitarian-humanist', says Frazer, 'can argue that, with all of its problems':

> the 'carceral' society described in *Discipline and Punish* is *better* [my emphasis] than the dictatorship of the party-state, junta or Imam; that, *pace* Foucault, the reformed

prison is preferable to the gulag, the South African or Salvadoran torture cell, and Islamic 'justice'; and that in this world – which is the *real world* [my emphasis] – humanism still wields its share of critical, *emancipatory punch* [my emphasis] (Frazer 1985: 177).

No doubt this is what can be argued and has in fact been argued innumerable times – that it is better. The argument raises a whole host of questions however, and the answers to them are not as simple as Frazer seems to think. What is good and what is evil, who defines them, for whom? Is there a distinction to be made between two, not a conceptual distinction to be sure but precisely a distinction that is viable in the 'real world'? Nietzsche famously said there is no such distinction and we have noted that the gift of European thought is also an insult, a gift of poison. This is the only way to make sense of the contradictory nature of postcolonial discourse, its intention to criticise persistently what it cannot not want. It is the only way to make sense of all critical discourses and forms of resistance for whom the object of critique is also an object of desire. We will not enter into this debate here however, as it will take us far afield. The question that we and Frazer in her own text have raised and seek to address is different. It is whether the 'longstanding Western tradition of emancipation via rational reflection' (Frazer 1985: 166) has anything to offer, whether emancipation is possible through such means. It should be clear that Frazer's utilitarian humanist is operating with what we have been calling here the liberal conception of power – that which presses on the subject from without. In fact, this persona is operating with the most sensational form that this power takes, for maximum effect no doubt – physical violence. As such, the argument does not even address the question of power as something that also forms the subject. And because it does not, it has nothing to say about the prospect of subjects constituting themselves as autonomous beings by thinking for themselves. In the 'real world' the humanism of the 'longstanding Western tradition' wields no 'emancipatory punch' at all. Nor, it has to be said, has anyone punched it in turn. No one can. It is immaterial (in the double sense of this term), a spectre or phantom.

We can anticipate another objection closely related to Frazer's claims about the real world. It could be argued that although autonomy may be an unrealizable ideal, this does not mean that everyone is subject to the powers that be to the same extent. Individuals or societies can be more or less autonomous or relatively autonomous, the same way in which an epistemic subject can be more or less objective and a discourse more or less true. Hence, it could be further argued, even if we restrict ourselves to the type of power under consideration – as that which forms the subject rather than what presses on it from the outside – the modern subject is still better off than its traditional counterpart. It thinks for itself more, questions things more or questions more things and hence enjoys a greater degree of autonomy. As we have seen, this is the argument made by, among others, all those in academic circles who realise that they are caught in a circle, recognise the impossibility of objectivity and/or autonomy but are not willing to accept it as the last word on the matter. The argument takes back to the question of time as the present, the now, this moment or instant and of the present as the gift – the auto-gift of autonomy that the thinking subject is presumed to give itself. This gift is said to be more of a present or more present in the modern world and less of a present or less present in the non-modern world. But it cannot be. If anything, the reverse is the case. Anything more than an instant is already caught up in the economy of time, which is to say, it has already become an object of anticipation and memory or representation in general. It is therefore less (a) present rather than more, at a greater temporal distance from the subject that wishes it to be as close at hand as possible – either in a future that has not happened yet or in a past that has already happened and is no longer present. We have already phrased this in a slightly different way. As we have said, the more autonomous a subject strives to become the less autonomous it is. In an instant, but one still caught in the economy of time, it generates all sorts of dependence – on the idea, those who propagate it, the culture that supports it, the social order that the culture legitimises and so on. The reverse is also true. Anything less present is in *a certain sense* more present, closer to the subject that does not represent to itself as much, that is, does not anticipate it hence place it in the future or does not remember it hence place it in the past. To put it in another way: the less autonomous a subject strives to become, the less committed to the idea, those who propagate it, the culture that supports it and so on, hence the less dependent on them. There is then no substance to this argument. On the contrary, if there is an argument to agree with, this is the well-known minimalist maxim: more is less and less is more. One would have to say that the more something is, the less it is and that the less it is, the more it is, so much so in fact that at the limit the most is also the least and everything (Being) is nothing. On this fundamental point, one would have to agree with Hegel after all or, at any rate, with one of his 'spectres'.

This structure applies not only to autonomy and heteronomy but also to all the other dichotomies we have been discussing – thinking and not thinking for oneself, resistance and consent, the modern and the traditional. To say this is not to deny the *phenomenological* difference between the modernist or Western subject and its non-Western counterpart, the same way that, as we have seen, one cannot deny the phenomenon of the gift or the phenomenological difference between the market economy and the economy of gift-exchange. On the contrary, it is to highlight it. There is no doubt that the modernist subject thinks that it thinks for itself, that it questions and doubts rather than conform, that it is more autonomous than its traditional counterpart. To put it in another way, the modernist subject is busy with these ideas – it thinks about them, talks about them, makes an issue of them, perhaps the most fundamental issue, the core of its personal and cultural identity. It anticipates autonomy – in a future that it presumes will become present, indeed, often said to have already become so; and it 'remembers' it being present at a time which it presumes was present – as we have seen in the last chapter, in aboriginal society, at the beginning of time, the state of nature. Yet this *phenomenon* of autonomy is enough to destroy it as autonomy. As soon as it appears, autonomy itself disappears. The modernist subject is no more autonomous than the traditional subject is dominated. The more autonomous it appears, the less autonomous it is. And the other way round: the less autonomous the traditional subject appears to be, the more autonomous it is – in a certain sense, as we have said, from the point of view of an imaginary external observer. It is more autonomous in this restricted sense if only because for this subject autonomy is not an issue. But of course, if it is not relevant it is culturally invisible, hence not present. Any way one looks at it, there is no such thing as autonomy. If it appears, it instantly disappears and is not present. If it is culturally invisible it is because it does not appear, hence it is not present either. Whether we like it or not, whether we are prepared to accept or not, no one is or can ever be free. Everyone lives on borrowed time, and because it is borrowed there is always already a price to pay for anything that anyone does in time and in the meantime – a cost of living.

The Cost of Living

We are accustomed to thinking of the cost of living in a rather narrow technical sense. To be sure this is how it was conceived to begin with, but there is no reason why we should restrict this notion to what happens in the market economy. We think of the *cost* in monetary terms and of the *living* in terms of the material and symbolic goods and services consumed – from food and housing to health and entertainment, to mention only some of the categories that economists use to calculate the cost of living index. One could say, therefore, that the cost of living refers to what it *takes* to live according to a certain socially defined and prescribed standard, what and how much one needs to take to achieve this standard and how much one must give in return. Yet living can hardly be reduced to the consumption of commodities. Nor can economy be reduced to the market, cost to monetary value, or taking and giving to the historical process that made the market economy possible – the division of labour. It always takes to live irrespective of the kind of living in question or the degree of the division of labour. And because it always takes, it also always gives. One could even say that living is in a fundamental sense taking or that taking is the condition of possibility of all living, of life itself.

The virtue of this model, then, is that it contains a structure of universal applicability, even if its wider significance is all but lost in the confines of economic rationality. It is certainly lost on the modernist subject, which still imagines that certain aspects of living, such as thinking or being politically engaged cost nothing and can be done for free – a gift, as we have said, that one makes to oneself auto-generously and auto-nomously. We shall try to recover the wider significance of the model in what follows. We shall take it as an axiomatic proposition that no one has, or can ever have what it *takes* to live. For it does take to live and everyone must take. Not even the life that one makes by taking is one's own property. This, too, is given, which is another proof, if another proof is needed, that dispossession and therefore dependence describe the nature of the human condition.

Something of the sense of finitude and dependence that we are trying to describe here, of the need to take what is not one's own – for by definition one is dispossessed – hence the need also to make amends for taking survives in language. The older meaning of the verb *to pay* is to appease or to pacify, from the Latin *pax*, meaning *peace*. One presumes that there is a need to pay in this sense because the subject is well aware that it appropriates what does not belong to it, that in taking, one transgresses natural, moral, or religious boundaries. It must therefore give something back, in the hope that it would be sufficient to mollify the powers that be, restore the order of the world, and maintain the peace. This phenomenon is attested in the anthropological literature of the nineteenth and early twentieth century on discussions of animism, the belief in other words that animals and plans are endowed with spirit. For many cultures in the world taking the life of plants and animals to sustain human life requires appeasement of their spirit or of spirits in general, and the phenomenon was reported widely in anthropology, no doubt, as an example of the 'credulity' of the natives and the primitive state of their intellectual condition.[4] As I have shown elsewhere (Argyrou 2005), such reports have recently resurfaced, this time in the environmentalist literature, but for an entirely different purpose. They are now presented as examples of the ecological wisdom of native populations, of an ethic of respect for nature that everyone, the West in particular, ought to adopt. Even so, the meaning of payment as appeasement and pacification has long been lost. Paying is what one does in the market for the acquisition of commodities. It is a contractual obligation regulated by the state, which also keeps the peace. As for life outside the market, there is a sense, and a fundamental one at that, that it is or can be made free – making a free living or living for free – a life with no costs involved, nothing to pay. Yet absolutely nothing is free. Even things that belong to no one and are presumed to be freely available to everyone – vital things, such as the air we breathe – are not free. There is a price to pay for them also. Consuming them life consumes itself, which makes death the ultimate cost of living.

It is a matter of some interest, therefore, to understand why and especially how the modernist subject convinced itself that life can be free, even though we will not pursue the issue here as it will takes far afield. It ought to be of interest not just to those 'drawn to the historically mediated concept of autonomy', as

Hinchman notes, but to everyone because it flies in the face of every possible experience:

> For those drawn to the historically mediated concept of autonomy, it is no longer a matter of theorizing from 'within' the horizon of autonomy but of explaining why, in rather specific contexts, Europeans *were ever misled into imagining* that they could direct their own lives, set their own rules, and find a place to stand outside of all power/knowledge complexes (Hinchman 1996: 489; my emphasis).

As we have said, we shall not pursue the question as to why Europeans were misled into imagining things. Perhaps the phantom of autonomy that gave itself to them to think about misled them into believing that it is a real being. But it is equally possible that they misled themselves. Whatever the case, the aim of this book has been simply to bring to as sharp a focus as possible these imaginings and to underscore the fact that contrary to how they have been presented over the last few centuries and no doubt will continue to be presented in the future, this is precisely what they are: figments of the imagination – which, as we have said several times already, is not to criticise them for being phantoms. It is the masque of reality and hence familiarity they are made to wear that needs to be removed, however frightening what lies behind it may turn out to be.

We have already noted that life cannot be reduced to the consumption of commodities. It is consumption itself (and of itself), expenditure of what one does not have and must take – which is everything – an expenditure that in the process expends the life for the sake of which there is expenditure to begin with. We have also noted that economy cannot be reduced to the market or cost to monetary value, and we shall try here to flesh out these claims partly by way of recalling some of the things we have said before. In the third chapter of this book we treated thinking itself as part of life (and to put it in this way is no doubt to state the obvious), under the rubric of economy and discussed the costs involved. We treated thinking as an economy, not for rhetorical effect or because of a penchant for neologisms but to stay as close as possible to the spirit and the letter of European thought and to highlight the inconsistencies – or the points at which European thought veers off course and begins to imagine things. As we have shown, it was European thought itself that treated thought economically firstly, by drawing a firm knowledge production-possibility boundary and secondly, by positing the impossibility of giving and receiving gifts of thought. But it was European thought also that denied the economy of thought by positing subjects capable of thinking un-economically or a-economically, that is, freely, without any constrains, outside the boundaries that it itself posited – subjects that could give themselves auto-gifts of thought. Hence the question of objectivity in the social sciences, which is still an issue, however low-key it might be in the current intellectual climate. We have argued that there can be no objective subjects, that the whole idea is a contradiction in terms. The subjectivism of the epistemic subject – the inability to give without taking back with a certain interest, hence the inability to be disinterested – is inescapable. It is the price that the subject has to pay for what it has always already taken and uses to think with. It is one of the costs of living – the cost of thinking.

In the same chapter, we noted the striving of the subject to find ways and means to avoid paying this cost – a form of intellectual tax evasion, so to speak. And we noted also that this striving is in a certain sense understandable. In the market economy too, the consumer strives for the highest possible standard of living at the lowest possible cost. What would be strange from the point of view of the market economy, however, is the epistemic subject's assumption or presumption that it is possible to think without having to pay anything. Consumers maintain no such illusions. They may move from one place to another to take advantage of differences in the cost of living, but they have no expectations to find a place where it costs nothing to live. Everyone knows that there is no such place, that no matter where anyone goes there will always be costs, in short, that there is no such thing as living for free or free living. The epistemic subject by contrast expects otherwise. As we have seen, for a long time it was assumed that it was capable of moving from where it was positioned and conditioned to a place where it could think without having to take anything and hence without having to give anything in return. It was assumed that it could detach itself from the economy of life and become a free-floating, free-thinking, objective subject. It is true that there are not many today who would be prepared to make such claims, at least not in so many words. Nonetheless, there is no doubt that the illusion of objectivity persists. There are still 'invitations to reflexive sociology' circulating and those who take them and take them up find out that there are 'three types of biases [which] may blur the sociological gaze'. The first is the bias of 'the *social* origins and coordinates (class, gender, ethnicity, etc.)'; the second concerns the position of the sociologist in 'the *academic* field'; and the third is 'the *intellectualist* bias which entices us to construe the world as a *spectacle*' (Bourdieu and Wacquant 1992). Can these biases be completely eliminated? Probably not, the sociologists would say, but they would also argue that this does not make objectivity an illusion. The thinking subject can be more or less objective, and that if it keeps in mind these three biases it is likely to be more rather than less. Yet this is precisely the illusion. As we have shown, more is less and less is more.

In the fourth chapter we turned to another aspect of living that escapes the market and all quantification, whether monetary or otherwise, and treated it in a similar manner – as an economy. We examined libertarian activity of different kinds – from revolution to the more modest engagement with power by identity politics, namely, resistance. We treated these practices as a political economy, understood as limitation to what can be done to liberate oneself and what not – an action-possibility boundary; and as exchange or circle where whatever is done always already comes back and confirms the politically engaged subject in its dominated position. Once again, the terms and concepts used in the analysis have nothing to do with a penchant for neologisms. We treated political action as an economy precisely because this is how it is experienced by those involved in it. As it is attested in the literature on liberation, the modernist subject has come up against the limitations and circularity of political action time and again, recognises them as such and is reconsidering its position, even revising its expectations. Or, to be more precise, it stumbled upon them and, given the culture in which it is steeped, was taken by surprise to find them in its way and does not quite know what to do about them. It cannot ignore them and pretend that they do not exist but neither can it accept them as the last world on the matter. As we have seen, much like the economy of thought, the political economy is both asserted and denied at the same time, the circle recognised all the while the encircled subject is looking for an exit. The aim of this chapter then, was to highlight the action-possibility boundary of this economy, to mark the circle and to show that there is no exit to it. Contrary to what the politically engaged subject might expect, in this domain too there is no living for free or free living, no such thing as autonomy, not even relative. Here, too, there is a price to pay for living and doing, a cost that may have nothing to do with monetary value but is not for this reason any less real. If for the epistemic subject the cost of thinking is subjectivism, for the politically engaged subject this cost is subjection.

All this might lead one to assume that what we wish to do here – at the end of this discussion of the gift of European thought – is to argue that European culture is on a trajectory of possibly irreversible decline. After all, such an argument has been made many times before both from within Europe and from without. Yet this is not our intention, nor is it what the analysis that we have carried out in this book suggests. Decline implies prior ascend, reaching a certain summit. Yet none of the things we have said supports such a hypothesis. If there is a figure that can accurately describe the movement of European thought since the Enlightenment this is none other than the figure of the circle. It describes it accurately to begin with, at the logical or structural level. At this level, one has to say that far from ascending any summits, European thought has been going round and round in circles from the very beginning, always already, by virtue of having been constituted the way that it has, even if it was too dazzled by its own light to take notice. The figure of the circle describes accurately the movement of European thought also at the historical level, the level at which one takes stock of how it all began and how it has ended. If one were to follow this trajectory – the discourses produced, arguments put forward, claims made over the last few centuries – the only possible conclusion to be reached is that European culture has come full circle: from preliberatory times – the time of the philosophers of the Enlightenment – when it was presumed that the subject was not thinking for itself and was therefore subject to the powers that be; to postliberatory times – our time, the time of, among other things, identity politics and the struggles for recognition – when it is recognised (and denied at the same time) that the subject cannot think for itself and is therefore beyond liberation. If one were to follow this trajectory, as we have tried to do in this book, one would have to acknowledge that the auto-gift of thought that the modernist subject gives itself in a gesture of auto-generosity and autonomy and the gift of thought which Europe gives to the rest of the world turn out to be nothing.

Notes

1. No particular kind of argument is specific for enlightenment, but its end is – which is desecration' (Bittner 1996: 352).

2. This is precisely the argument put forward by some of the radical factions of the environmentalist movement such as Deep Ecology (Argyrou 2005).

3. Thus in *The Philosophy of History*: 'Eastern nations knew that *one* is free; the Greek and Roman world only that *some* are free; while *we* know that all men absolutely (man as *man*) are free – [this] supplies us with the natural division of Universal History' (Hegel 1991 [1837]: 19).

4. Till lately some of the more credulous old men [the Indians of the Upper Missouri] declared that many of the misfortunes of their people were caused by this modern disregard for the rights of the living cottonwood' (Frazer 1963 [1922]: 129).

REFERENCES

Alexander, J. 1996. 'Critical Reflections on "Reflexive Modernization."' *Theory, Culture and Society* 13, no. 4: 133–138.
Arendt, H. 2006 [1963]. *On Revolution*. London: Penguin Books.
Argyrou, V. 2002. *Anthropology and the Will to Meaning: A Postcolonial Critique*. London: Pluto Press.
———. 2003. '"Reflexive Modernization" and Other Mythical Realities', *Anthropological Theory* 3, no. 1: 27–41.
———. 2005. *The Logic of Environmentalism: Anthropology, Ecology and Postcoloniality*. New York: Berghahn Books.
Asad, T. 1991. 'Afterword: From the History of Colonial Anthropology to the Anthropology of Western Hegemony.' In *Colonial Situations: Essays on the Contextualization of Knowledge*, ed. G. W. Stocking Jr., 314–324. Madison: The University of Wisconsin Press.
Bataille, D. 1988. *The Accursed Share: An Essay on General Economy*. New York: Zone Books.
Bauman, Z. 2000. *Liquid Modernity*. Cambridge: Polity Press.
Beck, U. 1992. *Risk Society: Towards a New Modernity*. London: Sage.
Benjamin, W. 1968. 'Theses on the Philosophy of History.' In *Illuminations*, ed. H. Arendt, 253–264. New York: Schocken Book.
Berger, P., and T. Luckmann. 1971. *The Social Construction of Reality: A Treatise in the Sociology of Knowledge*. London: Penguin.
Berlin, I. 1969. *Four Essays on Liberty*. Oxford: Oxford University Press.
Bhabha, H. 1984. *The Location of Culture*. London: Routledge.
Bittner, R. 1996. 'What is Enlightenment?' In, *What is Enlightenment? Eighteenth-Century Answers and Twentieth-Century Questions*, ed. J. Schmidt, 345–358. Berkeley: University of California Press.
Bourdieu, P. 1977. *An Outline of a Theory of Practice*. Cambridge: Cambridge University Press.
———. 1984. *Distinction: A Social Critique of the Judgement of Taste*. Cambridge, MA: Harvard University Press.
———. 1990. *The Logic of Practice*. Stanford, CA: Stanford University Press.
———. 1991. *Language and Symbolic Power*. Cambridge, MA: Harvard University Press.
———. 2000. *Pascalian Meditations*. Cambridge: Polity Press.
———. and L. Wacquant. 1992. *An Invitation to Reflexive Sociology*. Chicago: The University of Chicago Press.
Brown, W. 1995. *States of Injury: Power and Freedom in Late Modernity*. Princeton: Princeton University Press.
Butler, J. 1997. *The Psychic Life of Power: Theories in Subjection*. Stanford, CA: Stanford University Press.

Caputo, J. 1997. *Deconstruction in a Nutshell: Conversations with Jacques Derrida*. New York: Fordham University Press.
Chakrabarty, D. 2000. *Provincializing Europe: Postcolonial Thought and Historical Difference*. Princeton: Princeton University Press.
Chatterjee, P. 1986. *Nationalist Thought and the Colonial World: A Derivative Discourse*. Minneapolis: The University of Minnesota Press.
Collier, J. F. 1997. *From Duty to Desire: Remaking Families in a Spanish Village*. Princeton: Princeton University Press.
Comaroff, J., and J. Comaroff. 1991. *Of Revelations and Revolution: Christianity, Colonialism, and Consciousness in South Africa*. Chicago: The University of Chicago Press.
Cooper, R. 2002. 'The Post-Modern State.' In *Re-ordering the World*, ed. M. Leonard, 11–20. London: The Foreign Policy Centre.
———. n.d. *The Postmodern State and the World Order*. Demos.
Derrida, J. 1982. *Margins of Philosophy*. Chicago: The University of Chicago Press.
———. 1994. *Given Time: I. Counterfeit Money*. Chicago: The University of Chicago Press.
———. 1988. *Limited Inc*. Evanston, IL: Northwestern University Press.
———. 2006. *Specters of Marx*. New York: Routledge.
Douglas, M. 1966. *Purity and Danger: An Analysis of the Concepts of Pollution and Taboo*. London: Ark Paperbacks.
Eliade, M. 1959. *The Myth of Eternal Return*. New York: Harper and Row.
Fabian, J. 1983. *Time and the Other: How Anthropology Makes its Object*. New York: Columbia University Press.
Fanon, F. 1967. *The Wretched of the Earth*. London: Penguin.
Ferguson, N. 2004. *Empire: How Britain Made the Modern World*. London: Penguin.
Foucault, M. 1987. 'The Ethic of Care for the Self as a Practice of Freedom.' In *The Final Foucault*, eds. J. Bernauer and D. Rusmussen, 1–20. Cambridge, MA: The MIT Press.
———. 1996. 'What is Critique?' In *What is Enlightenment? Eighteenth-Century Answers and Twentieth-Century Questions*, ed. J. Schmidt, 382–398. Berkeley: University of California Press.
Frazer, Sir J. 1963 [1922]. *The Golden Bough: A Study in Magic and Religion*. New York: Collier.
Frazer, N. 1985. 'Michel Foucault: A "Young Conservative"?' *Ethics* 96: 165–184.
Gandhi, L. 1998. *Postcolonial Theory: A Critical Introduction*. Edinburgh: Edinburgh University Press.
Giddens, A. 1990. *The Consequences of Modernity*. Stanford, CA: Stanford University Press.
———. 1991. *Modernity and Self-Identity*. Cambridge: Polity Press.
Hamann, J. G. 1996a [1784]. 'Letter to Christian Jacob Krauss (18 December 1784)', In *What is Enlightenment? Eighteenth-Century Answers and Twentieth-Century Questions*, ed. J. Schmidt, 145–153. Berkeley: University of California Press.
———. 1996b [1800]. 'Metacritique of the Purism of Reason.' In *What is Enlightenment? Eighteenth-Century Answers and Twentieth-Century Questions*, ed. J. Schmidt, 154–167. Berkeley: University of California Press.
Hegel, G. W. F. 1971 [1907]. *Early Theological Writings*, ed. R. Kroner. Philadelphia: University of Pennsylvania Press.
———. 1991 [1837]. *The Philosophy of History*. Buffalo, NY: Prometheus Books.
Heidegger, M. 1996. *Being and Time*. Albany, NY: State University of New York Press.
———. 1997. *Kant and the Problem of Metaphysics*. Bloomington, IN: Indiana University Press.
Herzfeld, M. 1985. *The Poetics of Manhood: Contest and Identity in a Cretan Mountain Village*. Princeton, NJ: Princeton University Press.
Hinchman, L. 1996. 'Autonomy, Individuality, and Self-Determination.' In *What is Enlightenment? Eighteenth-Century Answers and Twentieth-Century Questions*, ed. J. Schmidt, 488–516. Berkeley: University of California Press.

Hoenisch, S. 2006. 'Weber's View of Objectivity in Social Science.' Retrieved 8 August 2012, http://www.criticism.com/md/weber1.html.

Hume, D. 1993 [1745] 'Letter from a Gentleman to his Friend in Edinburgh.' In *An Enquiry Concerning Human Understanding*, ed. E. Steinberg, 115–124. Indianapolis: Hackett Publishing Company.

Kant, I. 1999 [1781]. *Critique of Pure Reason*. Cambridge: Cambridge University Press.

———. 1991a [1784] 'An Answer to the Question: "What is Enlightenment?"' In *Kant: Political Writings*, ed. Hans Reiss, 54–60. Cambridge: Cambridge University Press.

———. 1991b [1786] 'What is Orientation in Thinking.' In *Kant: Political Writings*, 237–249. Cambridge: Cambridge University Press.

Locke, J. 1997 [1706]. *An Essay Concerning Human Understanding*. London: Penguin.

Lukes, S. 1973. *Emile Durkheim: His Life and Work*. London: Allen Lane the Penguin Press.

———. 2005. *Power: A Radical View*. Houndmills, Basingstoke: Palgrave Macmillan.

Malinowski, B. 1922. *The Argonauts of the Western Pacific*. London: Routledge and Keegan Paul.

———. 1926. *Crime and Custom in Savage Society*. London: Routledge and Keegan Paul.

Mannheim, K. 1936. *Ideology and Utopia*. San Diego: Harcourt Brace & Company.

Marx, K. 1963 [1852]. *The Eighteenth Brumaire of Louis Bonaparte*. New York: International Publishers.

Marx, K., and F. Engels. 1974 [1846]. *The German Ideology*. London: Lawrence and Wishart.

———. 1978 [1848]. 'The Manifesto of the Communist Party.' In *The Marx and Engels Reader*, ed. R. C. Tucker, 469–500. New York: W. W. Norton & Company.

Mauss, M. 1967. *The Gift: Forms and Functions of Exchange in Archaic Societies*. New York: Norton.

Mill, J. S. 1991 [1859]. 'On Liberty.' In *John Stewart Mill on Liberty and Other Essays*, ed. J. Gray, 5–128. Oxford: Oxford University Press.

Parry, J. 1989. 'On the Moral Perils of Exchange.' In *Money and the Morality of Exchange*, eds. J. Parry and M. Bloch, 64–93. Cambridge: Cambridge University Press.

St. Augustine. 1991. *Confessions*. Oxford: Oxford University Press.

Said, E. 1979. *Orientalism*. New York: Vintage.

Schmidt, J., ed. 1996. *What is Enlightenment? Eighteenth-Century Answers and Twentieth-Century Questions*. Berkeley: University of California Press.

Scott, J. C. 1985. *The Weapons of the Weak: Everyday Forms of Peasant Resistance*. New Haven: Yale University Press.

Spivak, G. C. 1991. 'Neocolonialism and the Secret Agent of Knowledge: An Interview with Robert Young.' Retrieved 30 August 2011, http://robertjcyoung.com/spivakneocolonialism.pdf.

Vico, G. 1984 [1744]. *The New Science of Gianbattista Vico*. Ithaca: Cornell University Press.

Weber, M. 1949. '"Objectivity" in Social Science and Social Policy.' In *The Methodology of the Social Sciences*, eds. E. A. Shills and H. A. Finch, 49–112. New York: The Free Press.

———. 1958. 'Science as a Vocation'. In *From Max Weber: Essays in Sociology*, eds. H. H. Gerth and C. Wright Mills, 129–156. New York: Oxford University Press.

Weiner, A. 1992. *Inalienable Possessions: The Paradox of Keeping-While-Giving*. Berkley: University of California Press.

Williams, R. 1977. *Marxism and Literature*. Oxford: Oxford University Press.

Yolton, J. W. 1993. *Locke and the Way of Ideas*. Bristol: Thoemmes Press.

Young, R. 2001. *Postcolonialism: An Historical Introduction*. Oxford: Oxford University Press.

Zizek, S. 2000. *The Ticklish Subject: The Absent Centre of Political Ontology*. London: Verso.

Index

A

agency, 16, 27, 105, 106. *See also* structure
    bind of, 107
    political, 108
Arendt, Hannah, 79–81
Argyrou, Vassos, 9n1, 40n6, 78n5, 110n2, 126, 130n2
Aristotle, 25, 29, 62
Asad, Talal, 20
auto-gift, 82, 124, 127
    of thought, 5–7, 17, 22, 36, 68, 84, 114, 130
autonomy, 8, 13, 19, 32, 37, 55, 59, 60–63, 100, 101, 109, 120–122
    as auto-generosity, 44, 130
    as a gift of thought, 5, 7, 9, 36
    and heteronomy, 117, 118
    relative, 76, 123–127, 129

B

Bauman, Zymunt, 64, 97, 98
Beck, Ulrich, 69
Benjamin, Walter, 88
Berlin, Isaiah, 63
Betaille, Georges, 35
Bhabha, Homi, 36
Bittner, Rüdiger, 55, 114–117, 130n1
Bourdieu, Pierre, 4, 8, 33, 90, 110n1, 122, 128
    and the gift, 30, 32, 40n9
    and the limits of thought, 75, 88
    on objectivity, 75–77
    on resistance, 95–97
Brown, Wendy, 89, 101, 102
Butler, Judith, 14, 102, 105–108

C

Caputo, John, 41–43
Chakrabarty, Dipesh, 10, 12–16, 17–24

Chatterjee, Patha, 40n3
Churchill, Winston, 37–39
circle, 1–9, 17, 20, 21, 32, 45, 56, 64, 66–70, 76, 77, 81, 84, 97, 105, 107, 108, 117, 121, 124, 128
    the economy of thought as, 55, 58, 60, 63
    full, 75, 129
    of political economy, 85, 91, 94, 101, 102, 104, 109
    vicious, 106
circularity, 1, 6, 32, 54, 57, 60, 64, 68, 80, 103, 106, 129
civilisation, 34, 37, 62, 99, 119
Collier, Jane, 40n1
colonialism, 6, 12, 34, 40n5
    critique of, 18, 19, 35
    end of, 19–21, 33, 100
    and postconialism, 110n2
conformity, 95, 109
    complete, 120, 122
    and freedom, 81, 118, 121
    logical, 57
    and resistance, 98, 99, 118
contradiction, 9, 27, 28, 42, 102
    in European thought, 8, 29, 61–63, 68, 71, 75–77, 87, 92, 95, 107, 108, 127
    in postcolonial discourse, 10, 11, 13, 16, 23, 24, 33
critique, 18, 19, 28, 43, 50, 51, 65, 86, 87, 94, 96–98, 99, 111, 113, 114, 123
    Foucault's definition of, 109
    of the metaphysics of presence, 41, 42, 52, 54
    postcolonial, 10–12, 14–16, 22, 35, 26
    of the pure gift, 29, 30, 51, 52
    of pure reason, 29, 40n7, 51, 52, 115
culture, 2, 38, 57, 65, 70, 72, 96, 105, 109, 111, 116, 119, 124

counter, 94, 97, 98
dominant, 94, 95, 97
European, 17, 35, 99, 129
non-European, 24, 104
oral, 62

D

death, 105, 126
    social, 1, 36
debt, 14, 31, 36, 84, 85
deconstruction, 41, 42, 51
democracy, 17, 50
    Derrida's view of, 53–54
dependence, 36, 114, 118, 126
    on Europe, 19
    on the powers that be, 84
    on society, 65
Derrida, Jacques, 17, 22, 25–32, 37, 39, 41–43, 45, 48–54, 84, 85, 87, 88, 97, 100, 117
desire, 14, 20, 33, 44, 45, 74, 85, 100–102, 105, 106, 109, 112, 120
    critique of the object of, 10–13, 15, 19, 22, 24, 123
    to give, 2, 39, 40, 44, 68
    for postcolonial revenge, 40n4
    to return to the beginning, 79, 80
despair; in identity politics, 101–106
deus ex machina, 27, 77, 89, 91, 95, 97
différance, 30, 53, 97, 100
domination, 89, 107, 109, 121
    class, 92
    colonialism as political, 12
    European, 104
Douglas, Mary, 8, 9n3
Durkheim, Emile, 21, 40n6, 63–65, 69, 105, 116

E

economy, 4, 5, 32, 124, 129
    market, 124, 126, 128
    political, 7, 32, 79–110
    of thought, 6, 32, 41–78, 129
Eliade, Mircea, 80
empire, 33, 34
    British, 38
    of darkness, 58
    as a good thing, 37, 39
    postmodern, 35
    Roman, 83
empiricism, 42, 63
enlightenment (and the Enlightenment), 6, 7, 19–21, 29, 41, 43, 44, 54–56, 58, 60–63, 112–119, 130n1
    humanism, 17, 18, 110n2

    motto of, 5, 59, 68, 111
    philosophers of, 6, 62, 64, 65, 69, 129
equality, 17, 19, 80, 99
    cultural, 21
Europe, 13, 14, 16–18, 20, 21, 23, 34, 98, 129, 130
    and its others, 24, 33, 36, 37
    provincializing, 10, 13, 15, 19, 61, 102–104
ex nihilo, 84, 108
exchange, 1, 3, 4, 19, 31, 45, 54, 60, 64, 83
    as a circle, 63, 84, 128
    gift, 2, 32, 110, 125
    symbolic, 30, 40n9
experience, 27, 45, 47, 101, 105, 119, 122
    beyond, 44
    possible, 28, 52, 53, 127

F

Fanon, Franz, 12, 13
feminism, 110n2
    first-world, 10, 11
    second-wave, 100
Ferguson, Niall, 34, 35, 37, 38, 40n10
Foucault, Michel, 105, 106, 108, 109, 120–122
Frazer, Nancy, 120–123
freedom, 27, 40n1, 81, 83, 85, 89, 105, 108, 110n3, 116–118, 120, 121
    as the aim of revolution, 80, 82
    from European domination, 104
    ideology of, 99
    intellectual, 60
    objective and subjective, 64
    sterility of, 9, 74

G

generosity, 3, 113
    auto-, 44, 130
Giddens, Anthony, 9n2, 61, 118
God, 3, 50, 76, 80
    individual as, 21
    and innate ideas, 47, 65
    knowledge of, 46, 48, 115
guardian, 59, 60, 62, 112, 119
    British newspaper, 8
    Kant as self-appointed, 112
    Society as collective, 68

H

Hamann, Johann, 62, 65, 78n6, 111, 112
Hegel, Georg, 119–122, 124, 130n3
hegemony, 64, 91–99
    alternative, 92, 93
    counter, 92, 93

Heidegger, Martin, 22, 23, 25, 28, 29, 63
historicism, 2–23, 33, 104
history, 13, 21, 42, 44, 51, 54, 76, 77, 91–93, 99, 102, 103, 115
    beginning of, 121
    of colonialism, 20
    as developmental process, 22
    end of, 53, 89, 121
    European, 17, 104
    of European thought, 59, 61
    Hegel's philosophy of, 130n3
    making, 64, 75, 80, 81, 82, 84, 87
    materialist conception of, 89
    universal, 120, 130n3
    and Walter Benjamin, 88
    world, 83, 86
humanism, 123
    Enlightenment, 17, 18, 100, 110n2
Hume, David, 43, 77n

I
identity, 37, 68, 89, 118
    collective, 105
    cultural, 124
    European, 35, 36
    fixed, 102
    modernist, 14, 15
    politics, 28, 89, 90, 94, 95, 99–111
    of postcolonial critic, 14–16
    sexual, 102
ideology, 6, 36, 64, 69, 73, 74, 92, 110n2
    dominant, 97–100, 109
    The German, 84, 88, 90, 97
imagination, 20, 54, 87, 95, 97
    European, 13
    figment of the, 29, 53, 66, 77, 108, 127
    modernist, 8, 80, 113
    sociological, 120, 122
imperialism, 10, 17–19, 33
    postmodern, 34, 35
    sociological, 63
impossibility, 26, 29, 82, 87, 110n2, 112
    of decentring Europe, 103, 104
    of freedom, 81, 116, 124
    of the gift (and gift of thought), 4, 5, 17, 25, 31, 39, 43, 44, 56, 127
    of objectivity, 75, 124
    of presence, 98, 111
    of thinking for oneself, 111, 118, 119
independence, 5, 19, 37, 76, 77, 98. *See also* autonomy; freedom
    political, 12, 16
instant, the, 3, 8, 25–27, 31, 54, 65, 67, 95, 106, 111, 117, 124

J
justice, 38, 41, 42, 50, 54, 77n, 100
    Islamic, 123
    social, 17

K
Kant, Immanuel, 5, 6, 25, 28, 39, 40n7, 43, 45, 47, 48, 69, 95, 108, 118–120
    critique of, 62, 63, 65, 111–115
    and enlightenment, 44, 55–61
    and pure reason, 29, 51–53
Kipling, Rudyard, 35, 39
knowledge, 5, 6, 41, 42, 57, 59, 64, 103
    absolute, 120
    limits of, 44–46, 48–51, 53, 62, 67–69, 71
    and power, 127
    sociology of, 66, 73
Kula, 1–3, 7, 26

L
liberation, 64, 73, 89, 129
    beyond, 7, 107, 108, 130
    as a meaningless slogan, 97, 98,
    from superstition, 115
life, 1, 15, 59, 63, 64, 68, 73, 80, 82, 84, 85, 87, 94, 98, 103, 125–128
    cycle, 2
    everyday, 4, 25, 51, 66, 69
    of the mind, 47
    rural, 99
    tribal, 3
    ways of, 20, 23, 118
limit (limitation), 3, 7, 8, 14, 31, 86, 118–120, 124
    economy as, 32
    of European thought, 13, 43
    of first-world feminism, 10, 11
    to knowledge/thought, 32, 44–46, 49, 50, 51, 54, 55, 63–65, 67, 75, 88, 119, 122
    to political action, 32, 84, 89, 92–94, 97, 99, 128, 129
    to postcolonial discourse, 14
    to productive capacity
Locke, John, 39, 43, 45–52, 54–60, 64, 65, 69, 78n2,3, 86, 97, 99, 117
Lukes, Steven, 40n6, 63, 105, 109

M
Malinowski, Bronislaw, 1–4, 6, 7, 26, 39, 123
man, 2, 8, 9, 12, 13, 48, 49, 54, 56–58, 60, 73, 75, 80, 88, 99
    white, 5, 13, 35, 39

INDEX • 137

Mannheim, Karl, 66, 73–75, 85
Marx, Karl, 23, 63–65, 69, 75, 81–92, 95–97, 99, 102
Mauss, Marcel, 1, 30, 36, 37, 39, 56, 133
metaphysics,
    of absence, 42, 43, 52
    of presence, 28, 41, 42, 49, 52, 53
modernity, 20–24, 40n1, 61, 62, 100, 117–125
    rejection of, 102, 103

N
nature, 49, 67, 77, 125, 126
    gift of, 46, 47, 63, 65, 76
    human, 2, 61
Nietzsche, Friedrich, 101, 123
nothing/ness, 3–8, 11–14, 17, 18, 24–28, 30–33, 37, 39, 40, 42, 44, 47, 48, 57, 66, 84, 119, 122, 124, 130

O
oikonomia, 4, 32
Orient, the, 35–37

P
paradox, 2, 11, 24, 62, 63, 100
    of conformity as the condition of autonomy, 7
    of conformity as the condition of resistance, 27, 98, 99
    of difference as the condition of sameness, 21
    of freedom as the end of agency, 74
    of imposed freedom, 116
    of subjection as the condition of agency, 105
    of taking by giving, 37–39, 113
    of taking for granted as the condition of thinking for oneself, 6, 113
    with time, 27, 30
Parry, Jonathan, 40n2
phantom, 41–54, 83, 95, 108, 113, 123
    of autonomy, 127
    of the gift, 4, 17–19, 30–32, 57, 98
    of objectivity, 75
phenomenon, 28, 41–54, 95, 108
    of autonomy, 125
    of change, 83
    of the gift, 4, 18, 31, 51, 55, 124
power, 27, 32, 56, 58, 60, 64, 74, 84, 95, 97, 110, 127, 128
    as condition of agency, 105–107
    of giving, 5, 32–40
    liberal conception of, 105, 109, 123
    structures of, 86, 90

present (the/a), 3, 5, 19–24, 26, 27, 29–31, 33, 39, 41, 42, 45, 50–52, 54, 55, 81–83, 85, 89, 91, 100, 106, 111–13, 117, 121, 122, 124
    future, 22, 25, 53
    past, 22, 25, 69
production, 26, 27, 67
    of critical discourse, 98
    instruments of, 99
    possibility boundary, 44, 84
        knowledge, 45, 49, 53, 62, 67, 127
    of wealth, 86

R
rationalism, 18, 63, 119
rationality, 2, 17, 42
    economic, 60, 125
reality, 13, 18, 47, 48, 54, 74, 87–89, 92, 96, 127
    accurate representation of, 117
    empirical, 28
    of human finitude, 77
    mythical, 95
    social, 64, 69
reason, 2, 3, 27, 45, 57, 61, 66, 75–77, 102, 119, 120. *See also* rationality
    good, 7, 13, 25, 47, 51, 71
    pure, 29, 40n7, 45, 51–53, 65, 115
receptivity; opposed to activity, 25–27, 92, 98
reciprocity, 30, 121
    cycle of, 14, 31, 85
    rules of, 13
relativism, 42, 43, 70, 73, 75
    cultural, 13, 103
    ethical, 42, 50, 51
reproduction, 26, 29, 52, 82
    mechanical, 27
resistance, 16, 19, 99, 106, 123, 128
    anticolonial, 16
    and conformity, 98, 118, 124
    peasant, 93
    to power, 27, 107
revolution, 7, 75, 79–91, 92–95, 99, 128
    American, 79, 81
    bourgeois, 86–90
    counter, 80
    English, 86
    Enlightenment as, 7
    French, 79, 86
    Glorious, 79
    Industrial (first), 21
    modernist, 80
    proletarian, 82, 84, 90, 91
    the spirit of, 85–87, 91

S

Said, Edward, 35, 36
Saint Augustine, 25, 29, 30, 54
scepticism, 51, 73, 77n
science, 18, 57, 102
    cultural, 71–73
    social, 56, 62–67, 69, 70, 73, 83, 127
    as vocation (Max Weber's essay on), 60
Scott, James, 95, 97–99
society, 3, 4, 13, 33, 42, 63–66, 68, 74, 76, 80, 84–87, 90, 95, 96, 98, 99, 105, 109, 111
    civil, 17, 48
    enlightened, 122
    modern, 32, 122
    original, 97, 121, 125
    traditional, 120, 122
sociology; of knowledge, 66, 73; reflexive, 128
spirit, 80, 83, 85, 92, 95, 120, 126, 127
    anticolonial, 15, 16, 19
    of critique, 43, 94
    of gratitude, 2, 16
    Hegelian, 82, 84
    nobility of, 39
    of the revolution, 85–87, 91, 95, 99
Spivak, Gayatri, 10–12
structure, 10, 27, 39, 52, 96, 97, 100, 103, 118, 124, 125
    and agency debate, 26, 82, 83
    of the gift, 19
    of power, 86, 90
    social, 122
    super-, 92
    temporal, 20, 21
struggle, 7, 16, 83, 86
    class, 97–99, 101
    for liberation, 84, 87–89
    for recognition, 129
    scholastic, 117
subject, 5, 6, 8, 9, 17, 26, 27, 30, 36, 37, 43, 44, 45, 58, 59, 61, 62, 69, 73, 75, 83, 97, 102, 110–115, 118–120, 127, 128
    conditioning of, 65, 67, 106–108
    epistemic, 6, 68–70, 74, 85, 123
    finitude of, 69
    modernist, 7, 76, 77, 101, 105, 108, 109, 116, 117, 124–126, 129, 130
    postcolonial, 15, 20, 21, 23–15, 105
    revolutionary, 84–86
    that thinks for itself, 53, 55–57, 60, 63, 66, 120
    traditional, 125
    transcendental, 72
subjection, 6, 20, 60, 64, 75, 105, 106, 129
subjectivism, 6, 7, 43, 68, 77, 127, 129
subjectivity, 14, 119, 120
    modernist, 15
    postcolonial, 17, 33

T

time, 2, 11, 21 39, 41, 42, 44, 45, 47, 50, 52–55, 62, 65, 81, 90, 100, 106, 111
    beginning of, 79, 80, 125
    borrowed, 68, 84, 110, 125
    Derrida's view of, 25–29
    historical, 20, 22
    mythical, 79, 80
    Saint Augustine's view of, 29–30
traditional, the, 5, 27, 40n1, 117–125
Trobrianders, 2, 3, 6
truth, 5, 13, 37, 40n9, 41, 42, 44, 50, 55, 53, 56, 58, 64, 69, 72
    as a gift of thought, 36, 63
    timeless, 49, 65
    touchstone of, 57, 61

U

unconscious, the; historical, 64, 69, 73, 74, 85, 111, 118

V

value, 3, 14, 20, 21, 36, 56, 57, 61, 63, 67, 70–72
    monetary, 125, 127, 129
    surplus, 37
values, 65, 66, 68, 70, 95–97
    cosmopolitan, 34
    liberal, 102
    Western, 42

W

Weber, Max, 60, 65, 101
    on objectivity, 69–72
West, the, 8, 18, 20, 34, 40n4, 126
Williams, Raymond, 92–95, 97

Y

Yolton, John, 48, 49, 51, 78n3,4

Z

Zizek, Slavoj, 12, 18, 100

www.ingramcontent.com/pod-product-compliance
Lightning Source LLC
Chambersburg PA
CBHW070045120526
44589CB00035B/2320